NEWTOWN

NEWTOWN

An American Tragedy

MATTHEW LYSIAK

GALLERY BOOKS

New York   London   Toronto   Sydney   New Delhi

The author is donating 2 percent of his advance and 5 percent of any subsequent royalties to The Avielle Foundation. To learn more about the nonprofit organization, please visit: aviellefoundation.org

G

Gallery Books
A Division of Simon & Schuster, Inc.
1230 Avenue of the Americas
New York, NY 10020

First Gallery Books hardcover edition December 2013

GALLERY BOOKS and colophon are registered trademarks of Simon & Schuster, Inc.

For information about special discounts for bulk purchases, please contact Simon & Schuster Special Sales at 1-866-506-1949 or business@simonandschuster.com

The Simon & Schuster Speakers Bureau can bring authors to your live event. For more information or to book an event contact the Simon & Schuster Speakers Bureau at 1-866-248-3049 or visit our website at www.simonspeakers.com.

Interior design by Jaime Putorti

Manufactured in the United States of America

10 9 8 7 6 5 4 3 2 1

Library of Congress Cataloging-in-Publication Data

Lysiak, Matthew
    Newtown : an American tragedy / Matthew Lysiak. — First Gallery Books hardcover edition.
        pages   cm
1. Sandy Hook Elementary School Massacre, Newton, Conn., 2012.   2. School shootings.   3. Sandy Hook Elementary School (Newtown, Conn.)   I. Title.
LB3013.33.C8L96   2013
371.7'82097469—dc23   2013034956

ISBN 978-1-4767-5374-4
ISBN 978-1-4767-5376-8 (ebook)

AUTHOR'S NOTE
ON SOURCES

I covered this story as a journalist for the New York *Daily News*, beginning on the afternoon of December 14, 2012. For the purposes of this book, I moved to Newtown. The story recounted here is a combination of my reporting at the time, hundreds of subsequent interviews, hundreds of emails obtained from friends and family members, and police documents, in addition to relying on various media reports I consider reliable.

Anything in quotation marks was either captured on tape, reported by me or other journalists, reconstructed from the memories of survivors, or published in official documents. Passages suggesting thoughts are in italics, and come either from emails, or in most cases, from the memories of the subjects themselves.

Actual names have been used, with the exception of one: the pseudonym Dennis Durant was invented to identify a person close to Nancy Lanza who was a frequent source but did not want to be identified. Due to the sensitive nature of the tragedy, relatives of Adam Lanza who contributed to this story also did not want to be named.

In several instances, conflicting accounts have emerged, including the timeline regarding which classroom Adam Lanza entered first and whether his initial target was Sandy Hook Elementary or Newtown High School. In both instances, and others, I move forward with the best evidence available at the time of this writing.

Quotes from Nancy Lanza and episodes involving her and Adam Lanza are compiled from the recollections of relatives and from emails either obtained or seen. No dialogue was made up for dramatic reasons or for any other purpose.

I refer to the press in the third person to avoid injecting myself into the story. In the initial fog of war, almost all media reports got major elements of the story wrong—myself included.

All time references for the attack are based on law enforcement sources along with recollections from eyewitness testimony, which at times have conflicted.

The morning of December 14, 2012, changed America. As we struggled to understand what could have been done to prevent the bloodshed at Sandy Hook Elementary School and, more important, how to prevent future tragedies, the country soon found itself embroiled in a national dialogue about society's role.

Much of the debate centered around our access to high-powered weaponry, flaws in our mental health system, school safety protocols, and the violent images that have become increasingly pervasive in today's culture. Sweeping legislation was discussed, new laws were debated, some laws were even passed, while other legislative proposals will still be debated long after the publication of this book. But while the country continues to debate what to do next, the facts of what led up to the tragedy still remain largely unknown. To have any hope of preventing the next Sandy Hook, we must first know the facts and circumstances that led up to the horrific act.

Who was Adam Lanza? Why did he do this? Could he have been stopped?

This book hopes to inform the debate and provide a broader context.

I believe this is an important story that needs to be told. Hopefully, this book contributes to a better understanding of what happened on that tragic day of December 14, 2012, and as a result better informs us on how to best move forward.

CONTENTS

CONTENTS

FOREWORD

By Monsignor Robert Weiss

When I arrived in Newtown in 1999, I was greeted with a variety of bumper stickers and license plate frames that read: IT'S NICER IN NEWTOWN.

That campaign carried on for several years, reminding us of what this community offers to its citizens. It is a town that has been through many changes in its more than three-hundred-year history, demographically, industrially, and socially. It is a place of quiet and respite where parents can raise their children with strong values and provide many opportunities for their growth and development into responsible and positive adults. It is a community where priorities are very clear, especially in terms of family, friendship, and faith. It is a community in which people choose to live because of who and what we are. And in just about every way, it is still "nicer in Newtown."

However, on December 14, 2012, the bumper stickers changed to: WE ARE NEWTOWN. WE CHOOSE LOVE as a result of the horrific action of one person that destroyed the lives of too many innocent people forever. There was no single victim as a result of that day; we all became victims.

We looked on in disbelief as more and more grim details emerged about what exactly had happened that Friday morning. The day started like so many others: parents went off to work with a hug from their children knowing that the weekend was almost here, other parents kissed their children good-bye as they put them on the bus or dropped them off at school, still others went about their chores knowing that the holidays were rapidly approaching.

As we all became aware that a horrible tragedy had come our way, rumors ran rampant and people began panicking. Events like this were not supposed to happen in Newtown; these things happened in urban communities, not in a town like ours.

I remember vividly the phone message telling me to come to Sandy Hook Elementary. Once I reached the firehouse, located a few hundred feet from the school, and saw the emergency vehicles and corps of first responders, I approached the front entrance of the building, usually teeming with happy students, and came to a sudden stop as I heard the sound of broken glass under my feet, a sound I still hear on sleepless nights. I stood frozen and quickly realized that I needed to be at the firehouse where the children and families were gathered. There, I found the real heroes of the day, the teachers and staff trying to calm the youngsters and create some order in the midst of chaos. Children ran to me, calling out my name. They were confused and afraid. They were not sure whether they should leave with their parents or stay with their classmates and friends.

And then the moment of reckoning took place as the parents of those students who did not respond to the roll call stood in absolute terror and were invited to enter the firehouse. The reality began to settle in. There continued to be hope. Rumors had it that some of the children had been taken to the hospital and some had run to the police station. Parents were on the phone asking relatives and friends to check anyplace they could think of to see if their child was there and safe. Frustrations and fears mounted as the passing minutes seemed like hours. One mother would begin to cry and another would console her. It was a scene no one could imagine, and certainly no one wanted to be a part of it. Then the announcement came, and one by one, parents, relatives, and friends were left holding tightly to one another, lives irrevocably changed.

Evil had visited our town. If for only a moment, we saw evil face-to-face as the lifeless bodies of twenty children and six committed educators were removed from a building that had been violated by one senseless action. The community was called together to be present for one another.

As I left the firehouse to return to the church and plan a vigil service, I was mobbed by the media. Question after question was thrown at me. Of course, the ultimate question was: Why? Why did this happen? Why did this happen here? Why were the lives of twenty-eight people destroyed? As often as the question was asked, there were no answers. I was also asked if the families were questioning why God would allow this to happen—a question not one person in that firehouse had asked that day. They knew this was not the hand of God. They knew this was evil.

Because we were in the midst of the Christian Advent season, the themes of this holy season became even more important to us: light overcomes darkness and good conquers evil. No matter what the circumstances, no matter how ugly and difficult, this truth was apparent. It only took seconds for the goodness of the community to emerge more fully than ever before—a goodness in each of us, now brimming over for everyone to share. People rushed to be with each other, holding something as simple as a tissue to dry the tears of those who were overwhelmed. As the early darkness of winter began to settle in, the light from candles began to light up the sky, thousands of candles. People gathered wherever they could. Simple shrines filled with flowers and teddy bears and angels began to appear. No one would be alone in this, no one would have to face it without help. We were in it together as a community and we were not going to let one horrifying action destroy who we were. Houses of worship were filled with people just sitting in stunned silence . . . and praying, perhaps for the first time in a long time. Could this be real? Could this really be happening? Where would we go from here?

Wakes and funeral services were planned. People gathered by the thousands to support those families who had lost their loved ones. Every service reflected love and care, the hallmarks of a town like ours. It was unbelievable to witness the outpouring of generosity, shared suffering, and true concern. It became quiet after that, as families retreated to their homes and entered that endless period of their lives filled with grief and mourning.

And then a new challenge emerged as Christmas Day approached. Should we just cancel Christmas this year? Should we extinguish the lights that decked our homes and businesses? Once again, the true nature of the town emerged. Christmas would be celebrated, although perhaps much differently than ever before. It seemed to me that the lights shone brighter, reminding me of the banner that hung on the front of our church: LIGHT OVERCOMES THE DARK!

People attended Christmas services in numbers that I have not seen in years. Families were holding each other more tightly than before. The celebration was about what really mattered in this town: faith, family, and friends. From all over the world, the town was filled with good wishes, gifts, cards, and prayers. We knew we were not alone and that we never would be. People could not do enough to help salve the open wounds that 12/14 had created in us—phone calls just wondering if we were okay, emails inquiring if there was anything that could be done to help, letters from people we will never know just assuring us that they shared our pain and grief. It was amazing, and it was wonderful.

Time has gone on. Some remain frozen in place while others are trying to move forward. Group after group provides support and counseling. Friends and neighbors continue to reach out to the families most affected. The town works diligently to plan for the future and provide a renewed sense of security for its citizens. Schools have reviewed their protocols for events like this to try and stop them from ever happening again, as we assure each other that we are doing the best we can to protect our citizens from harm, especially our children.

For me, this has opened a new horizon about my ministry and my place in this community. We are a community within the community. And I have been blessed to be called pastor of my parish.

Our families are strong and their faith enables them to raise children who are grounded in positive morals and values. I am always so proud when I pick up our local town paper and see so many of our parishioners involved throughout the community. We showed the world that in the midst of so much anguish, faith has a place in our lives. We continue to show the world that community is the answer; no one is meant to be alone or forgotten, especially in their times of greatest need.

As a priest, I am privileged to enter into the most sacred and intimate moments of people's lives, and this tragedy made that blessing even clearer for me. I stood in the midst of the purest love as I watched parents approach the casket of their child, and with tears, placing their hand to push back a lock of hair or place their child's favorite toy for them to hug all the way to heaven. That is love. That is courage. That is family. That is Newtown at its best.

A town that was once unknown to most of the world has become a part of the litany of towns that have endured tragedies. Smiles may still not be as plentiful as they once were but there are still hugs in the grocery store and words of thanks for just being there for one another. We are still "nice," and now maybe even "nicer in Newtown" as the bumper stickers originally suggested, but for new reasons. The one thing that I am most certain about is that we did not choose love simply as a result of 12/14; we live love every day.

Monsignor Robert Weiss, pastor
Saint Rose of Lima parish
Newtown, Connecticut

NEWTOWN

CHAPTER 1

——◇——

LAST GOOD-BYES

For parents, the chaotic hustle and bustle of getting their children out the door for school on the morning of December 14 was amplified for two reasons: it was a Friday and Christmas vacation was fast approaching.

In the home of JoAnne Bacon, the battle of the morning revolved around a tiny pink dress and a little pair of white boots.

"I want it! I want it! I want it!" pleaded her daughter Charlotte, her cute curly red hair bouncing to emphasize the seriousness of her request. A color has never matched a personality as much as bright pink matched Charlotte's. She had pink everything, including a pink dresser, and even slept in a big, pink four-poster bed. For the precocious six-year-old, pink wasn't just a color, it was a way of life.

JoAnne wasn't having it. The outfit had been bought specifically for the holidays and was the one thing Charlotte couldn't wear today, she argued. "You'll just have to pick out something else," JoAnne resolutely told her daughter.

But Charlotte would not be denied. The back-and-forth continued unabated for several minutes with neither party budging until finally JoAnne, sensing she was outmatched by her daughter's impressive powers of persuasion, realized the inevitability of the outcome: Charlotte walked out the door wearing the pink dress, white boots, and a large grin plastered across her face.

There were no arguments over what to wear at the home of six-year-old Jesse Lewis; Friday morning meant breakfast at the Misty Vale Deli where, at around 8 A.M., Jesse ordered his favorite breakfast sandwich—sausage, egg, and cheese—and a cup of hot chocolate before school. It had been a late night. Jesse had stayed up to go Christmas shopping with his father, Neil Heslin, buying gifts for friends, family members, and his beloved first-grade teacher, Victoria Soto.

The father and son began their evening of shopping at Stew Leonard's grocery in nearby Danbury. Jesse had $37 in his pocket, money he had earned by helping his father set bathroom tiles and fix their 1948 Ford tractor in hopes of having it ready for the next Newtown Labor Day parade so they could throw candy from the back. After carefully surveying the aisles, Jesse decided to use his money to buy Christmas ornaments. He picked out an ornament that had the word "Mom" on it for his mother, Scarlett, and a similar one that said "Brother" for his sibling, J.T. He then picked out two for his first-grade teacher, one a star-shaped ornament that read "Teacher" and the other in the shape of an apple.

"He put thought into it and was proud of the gifts he picked out," Neil later recalled.

The next destination was Walmart, where Jesse walked among the rows of toys to show his father the different gifts he hoped would be waiting for him on Christmas morning. He pointed at the Nerf guns, action figures, toy soldiers, and anything that had to do with the military.

The following morning, after finishing up his egg sandwich at the deli and before getting out of the car in front of Sandy Hook Elementary, Jesse turned and embraced his dad, saying, "It's going to be all right. Everything's going to be okay, Dad."

Neil didn't think much of it at the time. Just Jesse being sweet, he figured. Besides, they would see each other soon enough, Neil thought. They had plans to make gingerbread houses together later that day in school.

That Friday at the Barden household seven-year-old Daniel had some extra time before heading off to first grade. He had woken up especially early and had already played a quick game of foosball and devoured a bowl of oatmeal, so his father, Mark, decided it would be a good time to teach his son how to play "Jingle Bells" on the piano.

Mark Barden, a professional musician, sat close to his son on the bench and looked down at the small fingers as they pressed down on the keys.

The family was excited about the holidays and Daniel had already written his letter to Santa. Instead of asking for toys, Daniel just wanted to meet the big guy and his reindeer. "Dear Santa, I just hope you can let me see you with your reindeer. Merry Christmas. Please write back," he wrote in black marker. "I love you. Love Daniel."

The Bardens, like so many of their neighbors, were drawn to Newtown by the sterling reputation of the schools. They moved to town in December 2007, when Daniel was two years old, and older siblings James and Natalie were seven and five. The kids were in three different schools with three different bus schedules, which made getting everyone to the right school at the right time a challenge at times. Daniel's pickup time was the latest and he typically slept in while Mark walked his oldest son down the road for a 6:30 A.M. pickup.

But on this morning, as Mark and James made their way down the driveway in the dark, they heard the pitter-patter of little footsteps behind them. They turned around and there was Daniel, in his pajamas and flip-flops, awake before dawn to kiss his older brother good-bye. It was the first time in the three months since school had started that Daniel had woken up to say good-bye.

On the other side of town, another Sandy Hook family was busy preparing for the school day and, more important, the big party. Tomorrow was December 15, the day Josephine Gay would be celebrating her seventh birthday. Josephine, or "Joey Bear" as her dad liked to call her, loved to swim, so the family was busy planning an indoor pool party with all of her classmates. They had already made the cupcakes with icing in her favorite color, purple, and all of her friends had signed a special birthday T-shirt for her to wear at the party.

Joey's classmate Emilie Parker couldn't wait for the party either. The thoughtful six-year-old had found a very special present for her friend. Although Joey couldn't talk, suffering from autism and severe apraxia, her larger-than-life personality was readily apparent to Emilie, who refused to be satisfied with anything short of the perfect gift.

So Emilie's mother, Alissa, took her daughter to a local toy store where she roamed the aisles for thirty minutes. Desperation in her eyes, she looked up at her mom and said: "I just don't know which one to pick! It is so hard!"

Moments later Emilie returned with a Belle Barbie doll dressed as a ballerina. "Joey loves Barbies and she loves tutus. Joey can't talk, Mom. But she always touches my fluffy skirts and my Barbie backpack, so I just know she will love this!"

At home, Emilie put the gift for Joey in her closet, exclaiming, "I can't wait till Saturday!" She couldn't have been more pleased with her find. Inherent in her personality was the ability to make the most mundane tasks joyful, even when life turned stressful.

When the Parker family had moved to Newtown eight months earlier, they were still grieving over the loss of Emilie's grandfather, who had passed away that October. At the funeral, Emilie, a budding artist who carried her markers and pencils everywhere, slipped a card she had drawn into his casket. Making cards was something she frequently did to lift the spirits of others.

"She never missed an opportunity to draw a picture or make a card for those around her," her father, Robbie, recalled.

The Parker household was a place of love, affection, and constant learning. That December morning, Robbie had been teaching Emilie Portuguese before he left for work. Just before he walked out the door, Emilie looked at him and said "I love you" in Portuguese before giving him a kiss good-bye.

With Christmas only eleven days away, many children had already caught the Santa bug. And Jessica Rekos's Christmas wish list focused on one thing: horses. The six-year-old loved everything about the animal. She had been taking riding lessons at Kings Bridge Farm in Newtown and devoted all her free time to watching horse movies, reading horse books, drawing horses, and writing stories about her favorite animal. Her parents had even promised that she could have a horse of her own when she turned ten. This year she was hoping to find a pair of cowgirl boots and a black cowgirl hat under the tree.

They had to be "real cowgirl boots, not ones from Target," her mother, Krista, later recalled. With her hair in a ponytail and her favorite black glittery Uggs on her feet, Jessica marched off to school that morning not knowing that her parents had already fulfilled her Christmas wish and purchased her a pair of the prized boots.

Not every child was focused on Christmas: Benjamin Wheeler was focused on his future ambitions. Before leaving for school, the six-year-old wanted to convey an important message to his mother about his future: "I still want to be an architect, but I also want to be a paleontologist, because that's what Nate is going to be and I want to do everything Nate does," Benjamin said, referring to the older brother he idolized.

That Friday started out as equally happy and normal for so many other animated six-year-olds. The bright yellow buses crisscrossed through the narrow winding streets picking up students throughout the community on their way to Sandy Hook Elementary: James Mattioli, Ana Marquez-Greene, Catherine Hubbard, Noah Pozner, Jack Pinto, Allison Wyatt, and Chase Kowalski. Chase, a budding triathlete, came from his room wearing a green long-sleeved shirt, black sweatpants with a gray stripe, and black L.L. Bean shoes; his mother looked her mismatched son up and down before complimenting her "funny little guy's" sense of style. "Hmm, nice outfit," she told him.

The shy and tiny Madeleine Hsu, who always wore colorful flower-print dresses, and Caroline Previdi, an outgoing girl with beautiful green eyes, said their good-byes then hopped on the bus. Grace McDonnell skipped to the bus stop, unable to contain her excitement about getting to school. She always waited at the meeting point with her mom, Lynn, and the two of them would blow kisses to each other as the bus pulled away. That Friday morning, Grace added a pouty face for effect.

Dylan Hockley loved to run to the stop, too, playing tag with his neighbors along the way. Before the bus pulled up, he kissed his mother, Nicole, good-bye. Avielle Richman also waved good-bye to her parents after boarding the bus. Her mom, Jennifer, was standing on the porch and her dad, Jeremy, was in the driveway. Avielle flashed her gigantic grin as the driver pulled away.

And there was no suppressing Olivia Engel's joy either as the hours counted down to one of the final weekends before Christmas. After school, Olivia, who was active in her church's CCD musical program, was going to make her stage debut in the live nativity at St. Rose of Lima Roman Catholic Church in Newtown.

Olivia was going to play an angel.

CHAPTER 2

—◄◦►—

THE WINTER CONCERT

Dawn Hochsprung quietly sneaked into the school cafeteria to get a peek at her fourth-graders as they put on their Winter Concert dress rehearsal in preparation for the next day's big event.

"Aren't they amazing?" she whispered to a local reporter who had come to check out the event.

It was Wednesday, December 12, 2012, and the Sandy Hook Elementary School principal was overjoyed with her students' practice performance—so much so that she even took time to pull out her iPad to snap a few photos of the children in midsong.

"Sandy Hook students enjoy the rehearsal for our fourth-grade winter concert—a talented group led by Maryrose Kristopik!" she happily tweeted along with the picture of her schoolkids, who were all wearing white shirts and black bottoms as they belted out holiday tunes.

Dawn had held a deep affection for Sandy Hook and its stu-

9

dents since she first became principal in 2010. A big kid herself, on Pajama Day she would walk into school dressed in sleepwear with a pillow tucked under her arm, or wearing a blouse and a pair of pants inside out on Backward Day. In November, Principal Dawn transformed herself into the "book fairy." Dressed in a long, flowing, sparkling white dress and adorned with a golden crown on her head, the magical fairy went from room to room with her blue wand to thank the children for reading and sprinkle them with "fairy dust."

And she was always tweeting about what her students were up to, composing 140-character blasts like "Sandy Hook kinders write lists, select grocery items, and pay the cashier at Mrs. Vollmer's new Supermarket Center"—also attaching a photo of the children in the checkout line, cash in hand. The same year she was named principal, Dawn, forty-seven, told the *Newtown Bee,* "I don't think you could find a more positive place to bring students to every day."

As principal, she was seemingly everywhere at once, never missing an athletic competition or a school concert. She could often be spotted in the stands catching up on administrative work or with her nose buried deep inside a book. Principal Dawn also stayed up-to-date on the cutting edge of educational innovations. She had recently launched an "Appy Hour" to discuss mobile applications that supported school curriculum.

And positivity, it seemed, was something she consistently observed at Sandy Hook in the way of mantras. "I can. You can. We can. Because we can!" was just one of her many sayings that became known schoolwide. She outlined her aggressive educational philosophy in the "Sandy Hook Elementary School Handbook":

"Sandy Hook is committed to building lifelong learners, capable of responding to the changing needs and demands of our world. We hope to actively engage students in learning and help them become responsible and contributing members of our school community. Most importantly, we strive to ensure that our school is a secure, caring, and productive place for children and adults."

Few had doubts that she was succeeding. The delightful Dawn did have a reputation of high expectations and, as one Sandy Hook teacher put it, "If you didn't meet those expectations she would shoot you this look of daggers." Standing only five feet two inches tall, the petite principal "expected a lot out of her staff, but she expected even more out of herself."

Above all else, Dawn's expectation was to always keep Sandy Hook safe. "We can't control what happens inside their homes, but when they come here our children need to know that they are coming to a safe haven," the principal told one parent just a few days before the 2012 Winter Concert. "Without that internal feeling of security, all the teaching in the world won't make any difference."

Several new safety measures had been implemented at the school since Dawn arrived two years earlier. Before entering the building, visitors had to first ring the doorbell. Security cameras installed outside the school's main entrance let the clerical staff identify the person before hitting the buzzer and allowing them in. Once inside, parents had to show photo identification before going any farther.

"Safety first at Sandy Hook. . . . It's a beautiful day for our annual evacuation drill!" Dawn tweeted on the morning of October 17, 2012, along with a picture of six rows of children standing diligently in the school parking lot behind a line of orange construction cones.

The school also employed safety drills. Several times a year students and staff members would get into "lockdown," where teachers and children would lock their doors, find a hiding place, and remain quiet.

At the beginning of the school year, a letter outlining the new security procedures was sent to Sandy Hook families. "Our district will be implementing a security system in all elementary schools as part of our ongoing efforts to ensure student safety. As usual, exterior doors will be locked during the day. Every visitor will be required to ring the doorbell at the front entrance and the office staff will use a visual monitoring system to allow entry. Visitors will still be required to report directly to the office and sign in. If our office staff does not recognize you, you will be required to show identification with a picture ID," the letter stated.

After several parents expressed concern about young children walking home unattended, Principal Dawn launched new guidelines for children taking the school bus home. At a school board meeting in September, Dawn explained to parents the school district's new bus drop-off policy, which stated that students between kindergarten and fourth grade would be let off at the bus stop only if a parent or older sibling was around to walk them home.

If creating a safe learning environment was her first priority, a close second was caring for her devoted team of teachers and educational assistants and administrators, including special needs instructor, Anne Marie Murphy, and school psychologist, Mary Sherlach.

Anne Marie was highly respected for the gentle way she handled the children she looked after. The teacher was so beloved by one of her students, six-year-old Dylan Hockley, that he even kept a picture of the educator pasted to his refrigerator door. It was Anne Marie's ability to communicate with her students, many of whom had learning difficulties, that parents most appreciated. Many said the same of school psychologist Mary, too. She had an uncanny ability to patiently sift through a child's wandering sentences, pinpoint the problem, and quickly reach a workable resolution.

After eighteen years at Sandy Hook, Mary was preparing to retire following the 2012 school year to spend more time with her husband, William, at their home at Owasco Lake in the Finger Lakes region of New York.

But the fifty-seven-year-old would leave a band of talented new educators in her stead: Rachel D'Avino, a twenty-nine-year-old behavioral therapist who worked with children on the autism spectrum, and Lauren Rousseau, who had recently been given a full-time position as a "building sub."

Rachel appeared to be a perfect fit. As a child, Rachel struggled with learning disabilities but overcame them and went on to earn advanced degrees before landing a temporary job at Sandy Hook Elementary School, about a half hour's drive from her home in Bethlehem. Her first day at the new job was December 12, and that night she felt inspired to write a note for a time capsule to be read by a future generation.

"It is my DREAM that you know my name as a leader in behavior analysis for children and adults with autism. However, I will be thrilled if I make a few people have an easier, more enjoyable life."

Lauren Rousseau was already a familiar face to the principal. Dawn and her husband, George, had been longtime family friends of Rousseau, dating back to 1994 when George was her fourth-grade teacher at Roberts Avenue Elementary School in nearby Danbury.

Most in Newtown would describe the interconnectedness of the small-town school and the relationships between the principal, the faculty, the student body, and their parents with one word: familial.

On December 13, 2012, the night of the annual Sandy Hook Elementary School Winter Concert, the seats of Newtown High School's auditorium were packed with rows of parents, teachers, and members of the community who could barely contain their anticipation. All the big names from town were in attendance, including James Frey, the minority whip of the Connecticut House of Representatives, who had arrived to see his two nieces, Joan and Bridget.

Some students fidgeted nervously, while others stared blankly out into the open space. As the clock wound down, a hush fell over the audience. Music teacher Maryrose then paused, raising her arms, and the small mouths of every little boy and girl opened wide to utter a single unifying note.

The sound of Christmas echoed joyously throughout the hall.

"It was beautiful," Maryrose said. "Their voices lifted the entire room. It was just amazing."

The fourth-graders sang a number of holiday melodies. And at the concert's conclusion, the packed room gave the students a standing ovation. The performers bowed, beaming at all the familiar faces.

One face was missing from the crowd. Victoria Soto, the school's beloved first-grade teacher, was passionate about reading and decided she could not miss the local book fair taking place the same night. Victoria was another of Sandy Hook's most prized assets. Vicki, as she was commonly known, began her teaching career at Sandy Hook Elementary in 2010 as an intern. Dawn, however, gave Vicki her own first-grade classroom the next year in 2011 and she wasted no time in making the place her own, with her brother, Carlos, decorating the walls with learning tools such as the letters of the alphabet—large A-B-C cutouts in the shape of zoo animals.

The students loved the pretty young teacher who sometimes chewed gum during class and lined her desk with pictures drawn by her students, many inscribed with notes of affection like, "I love Ms. Soto."

On her Facebook page, Vicki wrote about her life:

"In my free time I love spending time with my black lab, Roxie. I love spending time with my brother, sisters, and cousins. I love spending time reading books on the beach, soaking up the sun. I also love flamingos and the New York Yankees."

Vicki came from a tight-knit family and embraced the role of mentor to her two younger sisters, Jillian and Carlee, often lovingly hassling them about their future goals and ambitions. That Wednesday evening, after discovering that her sister Carlee hadn't picked out her classes for spring semester, Vicki began teasing her, throwing papers and candy at her, jokingly trying to get her to start moving toward an academic future. She was also very close to Jillian, who had decided to travel to Vermont to go on a short skiing vacation with her boyfriend and two other friends.

It was 9 P.M. by the time Vicki returned home from the Scholastic Book Fair in nearby Danbury. Her mother, Donna, had dinner waiting for her. Vicki sat down at the table and showed her a Christmas present she had bought for her brother.

The next day was "Gingerbread House Day" for the first-graders' class, a day when parents were invited into the classroom to help their sons and daughters make the edible treats, listen to holiday music, and snack on baked goods. Vicki asked her mother if she could take some tissue paper to school to wrap the gingerbread homes at the end of the day to be given as holiday gifts to the parents.

"I'll go get you more later," Vicki assured her mother, promising that she would replace the paper when the family went on their scheduled shopping trip together on Saturday.

CHAPTER 3

—◄◦►—

ADAM LANZA'S FIRST DAY

On a fall morning in 2006, thirteen-year-old Adam Lanza was suffering through another anxiety attack. His face flushed red, his eyes opened wide through sheer force of will. Adam was determined not to suffer through another day of eighth grade at Newtown Middle School.

"I'm not going!" he screamed at his mother, Nancy. "You can't make me!"

Adam wasn't worried about the teachers or the schoolwork. He'd always been a good student and the schoolwork never proved much of a challenge. It was the thought of entering the massive building and confronting the hundreds of students who would crowd around screaming, talking, and running that had set him off.

"I won't go!" he shouted.

It was the type of showdown that Nancy Lanza had grown accustomed to. Her son Adam was first diagnosed at age five with

Asperger's syndrome, a form of autism characterized by significant difficulties in social interaction. Shortly after the diagnosis Nancy began telling friends that Adam had a second condition, sensory processing disorder, something the family would spend the rest of their lives struggling to understand.

Sensory processing disorder, or SPD, affects the body's sensory signals. The SPD Foundation describes the disorder as signals that are not organized into appropriate responses, creating a neurological traffic jam that prevents certain parts of the brain from receiving the information needed to correctly integrate sensory data.

Nancy Lanza turned on her calm, commanding voice and tried to reason with her son. "Adam, it will be okay," she pleaded.

It was no use. Her son wasn't in a state to reason with him. He was suffering.

"I'm not going," he repeated again, his voice rising.

It was a power struggle that would repeat itself nearly every day through the first few weeks of the school year. At times, Nancy was able to persuade her son to go, but more commonly it was Adam who prevailed and would be allowed to stay home and play his video games or spend time on his computer.

Throughout the struggles, Nancy tried to keep her son's issues in perspective. "Adam has been experiencing a lot of significant changes at home," she confided to a relative in September 2006. "This is his way of working through it."

And it *had* been a challenging time inside the Lanza household. Earlier that year Nancy had separated from Adam's father, Peter—again.

Nancy Champion was a senior at Sanborn Regional High

School in Kingston, New Hampshire, in 1978 when she first met Peter Lanza. Nicknamed "Beanie," the slender high school senior, with her inviting smile framed by long blond waves, melted over an older boy with "beautiful eyes" she met who had come from nearby Haver Hill High School in Massachusetts, fifteen miles north.

Peter Lanza was nicknamed "Mousey" in his high school yearbook, but his two brothers knew the shy, thin boy as P.J. He came from a modest upper-middle-class upbringing brought about from his father Peter Sr.'s income as a successful insurance salesman at John Hancock. Young and in love, the pair married three years afterward in 1981, though, in hindsight, Peter may have later realized that he'd overlooked Nancy's inherently assertive and litigious nature when, after the couple got into a minor car accident, his girlfriend complained of injuries and filed suit against him for damages. Peter's insurance company decided to settle.

The couple built a three-story Cape Cod–style house on two and a half acres of land on the six-acre lot owned by the Champion family next to the 1760s homestead where Nancy was born. The couple lived alone there for several years until 1988 when their first son, Ryan, was born on April 10. Four years later, on April 22, 1992, Nancy gave birth to Adam, a "beautiful, baby boy."

During those years as a new mom, she worked as a stockbroker at the John Hancock mutual life insurance company in Boston's financial district, while Peter went to get his undergraduate degree in accounting at the University of Massachusetts Lowell and then a master's in taxation at Bentley University. Nancy wound up filing suit against John Hancock, claiming the company discriminated against her after conceiving Adam; she said she earned consistently high marks on job evaluations for eight years, and it was only during her pregnancy—with bouts of morning sickness and other complications, including hypoglycemia—that her performance began to suffer. Nancy was forced to take a medical leave of absence while the company was going through departmental changes, but she was apparently told that she would still have a job after the restructuring. Just as she was about to return from maternity leave in 1993, Nancy learned she was among the employees who would be let go. She brought a suit against the company and the case was eventually settled.

In addition to winning this settlement, Nancy and Peter had their marriage blessed by tremendous financial success—Peter landed a highly paid position in Newtown with General Electric; so ultimately, the responsibility of raising the two boys fell primarily on Nancy.

The couple's clashing personalities made them seem an off pairing to friends: Nancy was vivacious and passionate, arguably too much so at times, while Peter was more private and steered clear of social gatherings, preferring the comfort of his work to the company of others.

"Peter worked all the time. He would leave for work before the children woke up and not get home until after they'd gone to sleep," said Nancy's friend Marvin LaFontaine. "Nancy never complained about it, but it was obvious that she had a lot on her shoulders. She was essentially a single mom, but that was something she took great pride in."

It wasn't long after making the move to Newtown that their

marriage began to fall apart. In Nancy's view they both had short-comings.

"Peter has the wonderful ability of being able to talk to anyone, and get along with anyone in the short term. He is definitely very focused on his career, and rarely socializes . . . but when he finds himself forced into a social situation, he does very well," Nancy wrote to a friend in an email on March 12, 1999. "Let's not confuse the ability to seem friendly and sincere with the real thing. He can chit-chat with someone and seem like best of friends, and then later say some of the most awful things about that person. It is pretty funny, really. One night I asked him if he could think of ANYTHING nice to say about ANYONE (personal . . . someone handling a business deal at work well would not qualify). He was silent for about five minutes . . . I thought he was ignoring my question. Finally he said, 'Reagan was a good president.' It took him that long to think of something nice to say, and even then, it wasn't at all personal! He has few friends . . . no hobbies . . . but he certainly excels at his job."

In another email she wrote, "Peter works incredible hours . . . he leaves at 5:00 to 5:30 in the morning and gets home usually around 10:00. Sometimes he comes home early . . . 7:30 . . . and sometimes later . . . 12:00. Major workaholic . . ."

In the same email thread, Nancy turned her critical eye inward: "I definitely am a very different person depending on the setting. I can come across as being very reserved in a group setting, but tend to relax more in small, intimate groups or with close friends. I tend to be more critical and judgmental . . . but I am like that all the time, not just in public or private. My dearest friends know that I am like that . . . some other, more distant people might take me for a bit of a snob . . . but who cares about them? The best thing (I think) about me is that if I don't like someone, I never feel the need to pretend or be fake about it. Everyone knows where they stand with me."

By 2001, now settled in Newtown for thirteen years, Nancy asked Peter to move out. He would move back in twice more over the next seven years, but the couple couldn't seem to make it work. Friends said it was Nancy who wanted the separation and eventually the divorce, which she filed for on December 9, 2008, stating that "the marriage has broken down irretrievably and there is no possibility of getting back together." According to court records Nancy checked yes for financial disputes but no for parenting disputes as reasons for the split.

Adam didn't take the news of his parents' latest separation well. He was also upset by the prospect of another move. Nancy had been openly contemplating moving to Avon, Connecticut, a town sixty miles upstate, which would mean a whole new environment for Adam—something he found deeply unsettling.

In addition, a growing distance had developed between Adam and his brother, Ryan, four years his senior. Unlike Adam, Ryan was socially well adjusted, one of the popular kids at Newtown High. He had recently gotten a car, too, and like most teens, began spending more time away from home, hanging out with friends. It wouldn't be much longer before Adam's popular older brother would graduate from high school and go on to Quinnipiac University, leaving him alone in the house with his mother.

Adam, Nancy explained to friends, sees the world differently. The tantrums were just his way of coping. Still, she noticed that the anxiety building inside Adam appeared to be gaining momentum. The outbursts were becoming more extreme, and what had started out as another typical episode that fall morning in 2006 had quickly morphed into something far more disturbing. Adam began hyperventilating and at times appeared unresponsive. There was something about his behavior that frightened Nancy. She was at a complete loss and feared her son was having a nervous breakdown. She corralled him into her car and drove him to Danbury Hospital.

Once in the emergency room, Nancy told the doctors that her son had been experiencing an increasing amount of anxiety. He was panicking at the idea of going to school and being placed in large groups of people. She also explained his hypersensitivity to touch caused by his sensory perception disorder.

Adam couldn't always recognize physical pain or hot and cold temperatures like most children, but he could easily be overwhelmed by the fabrics of his own clothes as they brushed up against his skin or the texture of food inside his mouth as he chewed. The slightest involuntary touch from another person was sometimes enough to make him withdraw for hours.

Nancy wondered aloud whether her son had outgrown what had previously been diagnosed as borderline autism into something much more extreme. "Something is very wrong with him," she told the doctor, imploring them to help her with her son.

The attending physician was not nearly as alarmed as the nervous mother. Adam had been handed a questionnaire to fill out. One question asked: "Are you suicidal?" He checked no. Another asked: "Would you hurt others?" Again, Adam answered no.

After the doctor had finished examining him, asking several

more questions while Nancy waited in another room, he concluded that the young boy wasn't a danger to himself or to others, and was free to leave. No medication was needed, Nancy was told, but she should be sure to follow up later with her family pediatrician.

Nancy wasn't having it and demanded an explanation. She had gone to school counselors, specialists, her family physician, and now an emergency room doctor, and no one could give her an answer—worse, no one seemed to be taking her concerns seriously.

"This isn't normal behavior," she insisted to the doctor.

Before leaving the emergency room Nancy asked for one more thing: a note to give to the school that would allow her to keep him at home for the remainder of his eighth-grade year. At home, Nancy believed, she could nurture her son into an improved state of mind and better prepare him for high school. The doctor refused.

It was clear from an early age that Adam Lanza was different. His aversion to social activities became apparent by age four. He rarely found enjoyment in playing with other children. The tot often tagged along when older brother, Ryan, went to Cub Scout meetings, only to separate himself from the crowd. He refused to engage in group activities and shrank away into the arms of his mother if another child touched him.

"It was obvious to everyone that as a child, Adam was different," recalled Marvin LaFontaine, who often helped out at Scout meetings. "There was a weirdness about him. He wasn't a normal child. Nancy would tell me: 'Don't touch Adam, he doesn't like being touched.' We all just thought he would grow out of it. He never did."

There was, however, one child his age Adam did not seem to mind. Jordan LaFontaine, Marvin's son, was one of Adam's only friends. Nancy and Marvin would often take the two, along with Ryan, to a fifty-yard stretch Marvin had carved out on his property where they would shoot an aluminum Ruger 10/22 at paper bull's-eyes and other targets in the shapes of woodchucks or crows. From an early age, Adam was comfortable with a firearm.

"Adam was four at the time he shot his first gun," Marvin remembered. "We enjoyed target shooting. We were safe . . . Nancy and I were very strict about it . . . She was very, very detail oriented and very, very strict with her kids about safety."

Nancy was always "fiercely protective" of her youngest son, checking and double-checking that he was wearing his safety goggles and earplugs before allowing him near the weapon.

The aluminum Ruger 10/22 was Adam's first gun. It was lightweight and easy to handle and, in Nancy's opinion, the ideal weapon for her young child. Adam's tiny face would tense up as he concentrated while his mother would patiently go over, step-by-step, the proper hold and technique for the small firearm.

"From the beginning you could tell that Adam liked the feel of the gun in his hands and that he was a quick learner," Marvin said. "When Adam was focused he could really focus and in no time he became a good shot.

"He seemed to really enjoy himself on the range—and Nancy, too. She would enjoy watching Adam as he would practice with the little rifle."

Nancy was a country girl through and through. She grew up on a farm with her mother, Dorothy, a school nurse at the local elementary school; her father, Donald, who worked as a pilot for TWA; her two brothers, James and Donnie; a sister, Carol; and a dozen kittens, chickens, sheep, and cows. (She painstakingly gave each one its own unique name. One particular hen was her favorite; she named it Phyllis Diller because of the big plume of feathers that came out of the top of its head.)

Nancy had developed a love of hunting from an early age and fancied herself one of the boys. As a young teen she would go out with her brothers in the lush acres of forest surrounding her hometown and hunt game. By the age of sixteen, she could skin her own deer. Her adolescent summers were spent playing in the great outdoors all day with her brothers, often with weapons.

"She came from a culture of guns. That's how she was raised in New Hampshire. Live free or die, that was the kind of woman Nancy Lanza was. She was an independent kind of woman," said Russell Ford, a friend of Nancy's. Dan Holmes, her landscaper, remembered, "Whenever I finished work she would invite me in for a drink; she spoke often about her fascination with firearms. She had an extensive gun collection, and she was really quite proud of it.

"One day I was over and she asked me to wait, then brought this really nice case out, and when she opened it up, she pulled out this old rifle. It looked beautiful and old. She would just smile when she looked at it."

Although Nancy loved to hunt and target-shoot, as a young girl she couldn't stand to see an animal in pain. When she was a kid, she told anyone who would listen that one day she was going to be a veterinarian. Once when her kittens looked unhappy, she was concerned and tasted the cat food to make sure it was okay for them to eat. Another time she took in a baby bird that was injured and tried to nurse it back to health. Then cried for a day before giving the small bird a funeral next to the tree it had fallen out of.

Nancy joined the 4-H Club when she was old enough, which was where she learned how to ride horses. And every year when the agricultural fair and circus came to town, she would furiously plot with her older brother Donnie on how they were going to free the elephants. When that didn't work, they would sneak them extra hay. (Interestingly, by the age of thirteen, Adam had adopted a vegan, organic lifestyle out of a moral concern, Nancy told friends. "He did not want to be the cause of animals suffering," she had explained.)

Nancy was known by her friends as a brazen child who had an adventurous streak. She would always speak her mind and was assertive about what she wanted. As a mother, she tried to project a confident and calm demeanor on the outside but, if she ever sensed her younger boy might be in danger, another side to her personality was quick to surface. While her oldest son, Ryan, was allowed to run and play by himself in the forest on Marvin's New Hampshire property for hours at a time without supervision, if Adam was out of her sight for even a moment a "switch could flip."

"Nancy was an intense personality; she could go from being mellow and soft-spoken to very upset, very quickly. Adam was associated with that side of her," Marvin recalled. "Some part of her became active if he was in distress."

Marvin experienced the darker side of Nancy's personality just once but it was a memory that forever stayed with him. On April 15, 1998, they had traveled together to Boston with the Boy Scouts' pack to see the Celtics in action at the FleetCenter. The group had a relaxed, enjoyable time during the first half. Nancy and Marvin were sitting together in the tenth row of the balcony, while Adam, who was days away from his sixth birthday, sat in the row directly in front beside his brother and Marvin's son, Jordan.

At the halftime intermission, with the Celtics trailing 57–48, Nancy asked Marvin to keep an eye on Adam while she went to use the restroom. Marvin turned his head momentarily and when he looked back, he realized that the boy had slipped away. When Nancy returned ten minutes later, she saw Adam's seat empty, and erupted.

"She was hysterical and screaming, 'My God, where is Adam?'" Marvin recalled. "I had no idea where he had gone, but I knew he couldn't have gone far and that there was no reason to panic."

Marvin looked at Nancy. She was hyperventilating; her face was beet red. She was so distressed it flashed through his mind that he might need to seek medical attention for her.

"It wasn't just a meltdown. It was an enormous panic attack," Marvin said. "I was tremendously worried. I didn't know what was happening. I had never seen her like that."

A few moments later, Marvin spotted Adam's scruffy red hair several feet away in the tunnel near the concession stands. "Little Adam was touching the walls with his fingers. I walked up to him and said, 'What's up, dude? You know you weren't supposed to leave your seat. Do you know what you just did to your mother?'" Marvin said.

But Adam was unmoved by the chaos he had caused and barely acknowledged Marvin's presence. He calmly turned around and returned to his seat as if nothing had happened.

"He just had this blank look in his eyes, as if he didn't know who I was or something. He didn't say a word. It kind of scared me."

With Adam safely back in his place, Nancy regained her composure and returned to watching the rest of the game, but her reaction that day resonated with Marvin years later.

"It hurt me terribly. I really felt like I let her down. I never saw that side of her before and never wanted to see it again," he said.

That same year, Nancy enrolled Adam in kindergarten, already well aware that she needed to be a champion for her son's challenges. She had the school district draw up an individual education plan, or IEP, in accordance with the students with disabilities act, to address his antisocial behavior, and hoped they could tailor his school day to better suit his needs.

When her husband, Peter, was named vice president of finances at General Electric soon after, the family decided to relocate to a small town in Connecticut called Newtown. Nancy Lanza saw the move as an opportunity for her struggling son to have a brighter and more stable future.

The people who live there often say Newtown in the fall resembles a Norman Rockwell painting. Branches with yellow and red leaves drape the Victorian homes of this quaint New England hamlet, and at the crossroads of its main thoroughfares—Main Street, Church Hill Road, and West Street—stands a single pole bearing the American flag. Legend has it that every road in Fairfield County leads to the pole, which has stood in the middle of Main Street since 1876.

Newtown is regarded as one of the safest towns in the country, so safe that families often leave their doors unlocked, but the town's main attraction is the sterling reputation of its schools, especially that of Sandy Hook Elementary. Located at the end of Dickinson Drive, a one-way street off of Riverside Road, and surrounded by lush hemlock and evergreen trees, the school is renowned for its high academic standards, routinely exceeding the state scoring averages in reading, writing, and math. It had also earned a reputation as a progressive school that was well equipped to deal with special needs students, a strong selling point for Nancy.

When the Lanzas arrived in 1998, they purchased a four-bedroom, three-bath Colonial for $405,900. A swing set with a small slide and a wooden fort was built for six-year-old Adam. In the backyard they had an in-ground swimming pool accompanied by a white wooden pool house on the 2.19-acre property. The young family couldn't have been more pleased with their first year in their new home.

"People are so nice here," Nancy wrote to Marvin, back in New Hampshire. "I feel very lucky to have found a place where there is such a feeling of community. It is beautiful here, and there is SO much to do and see."

Nancy loved the new house, and had plans to convert the basement into a room for her sons. "The game room is for the boys . . . it will actually be two rooms and a bathroom. In addition, I will have laundry room, exercise room for myself and perhaps a small shop area for my newest hobby (refurnishing antiques). There will also be a storage area that will not be finished off," Nancy emailed Marvin. "The boys are very excited about having a game room."

Another upside to the move was the "mild Connecticut winters," which were an improvement over winters in New Hampshire.

At first, Adam seemed to be adjusting well to the move. He excelled academically in every course. He was involved in other activities, too, including music, and especially drama. In emails to a friend during their first spring in Newtown, Nancy wrote glowingly of young Adam's blossoming affinity for the stage.

"Adam started in his theater group last week and enjoys it," she said in an email dated April 12, 1999. "It has been so cute to watch them rehearse. Adam has taken it very seriously, even practicing facial expressions in the mirror!

"Adam's first play went well . . . his second one is this afternoon with a second showing this evening. Watch out Broadway!!! The first one was a Charlie Brown play . . . today's is a smaller version of Oklahoma!"

Nancy was adjusting to her new surroundings as well. She had joined a local bunko group, where several of her neighbors rotated houses to play the popular dice game. She had also become a familiar face at Adam's elementary school, where she tried to spend as much time as possible watching over her son. The faculty enjoyed her presence, even offering her a volunteer job.

"We had Field Day at the school on Tuesday . . . I was in charge of the Tug-of-War . . . the kids showed up in groups of 40!!! At the end of the day, the gym teacher came over and offered me a job! She said that I was a natural for organizing large groups of children. Too funny!!! Naturally, I declined . . . but I was flattered," she wrote to a friend.

Spring in the Lanza household also meant birthdays for Ryan and Adam. Nancy planned a total of seven parties for her two sons in an effort to use the occasion to help her children better acclimate. "Ryan and Adam's birthdays are coming up," Nancy wrote to a friend on March 31, 1999. "It is making for a very busy month! Ryan is having an 'Old Friend' party and a 'New Friend' party . . . Adam is having only a 'New Friend' party . . . but he has 26 new friends!!! They will both have a family party and a school party."

While outwardly brimming with confidence, privately Nancy had already begun voicing concerns to friends that Adam's condition might be more serious than she had previously suspected. During Adam's sixth birthday party at Danbury Duckpin Lanes, a bowling center in nearby Danbury, Nancy confided to Wendy Wipprecht, the mother of one of Adam's classmates who also had special needs, that she worried about her son possibly suffering from a neurobiological condition.

"He's getting worse, not better. He needs help," she told friends. "He is remarkably intelligent but he struggles in so many ways."

The long-suspected diagnoses of Asperger's and sensory perception disorder (SPD) came soon after. Adam displayed all of the symptoms commonly associated with avoidant SPD; he flinched at sudden movements, recoiled from touch, sought seclusion, and preferred the dark.

The diagnoses made sense to Nancy, who for years had been struggling to identify what was wrong with her son. Adam was bright, with an uncanny ability to process information quickly, but the sound of running bathwater could drive him mad. Still, she told friends, Adam had been diagnosed with "borderline autism" and that it was "not severe."

In many ways, Adam seemed to prosper during his first-grade

year at Sandy Hook Elementary. He got great grades and attended normal classes with the rest of the children, but to fellow classmates Adam came across as an odd, aloof child who could never quite fit in. Adam stood alone at recess making animal noises, straining himself until his cheeks turned red. Others described him as someone who "scared the other kids." Another classmate remembered simply that "he always seemed so angry."

His second-grade teacher, Carole MacInnes, saw Adam as a quiet, intelligent child who did well academically and needed no special attention. "He was a frail little fellow and rarely spoke. There was a quiet depth to him that I couldn't penetrate, but there were no problems," she later recalled.

As a third-grader, Adam tried his hand at Little League baseball where his differences soon became apparent to his teammates. He would often stand at the plate with the bat on his shoulders as the pitcher threw strike after strike across the heart of the plate. Adam rarely swung, usually striking out and slumping back to the dugout where he sat off to the side by himself.

Nancy attended every game and practice, always keeping a close eye on her boy. To some of the other parents, her protective nature sometimes came off as extreme and overbearing. In one instance, as Adam was walking back to the dugout after striking out at the plate, another child passing by said, "Nice try."

Hearing the compliment, Adam looked nervous and quickly scampered to the dugout. After the game Nancy confronted the coach and demanded to know what the boy had said to her son. "She was paranoid that the other kids were bullying him but that just wasn't the case, at least in this instance," one parent recalled. "Most of the kids just ignored Adam."

One former teammate had a different recollection of Adam's time in Little League, remembering him as "not a good player."

"Some kids picked on him, making fun of him. He'd always get put in the outfield where he wouldn't see a lot of action. I remember one time he was hit by a pitch that knocked him over. Someone said he couldn't feel any pain so what's it matter anyways and everyone kind of laughed. I felt kind of bad but he didn't even try to fit in. He ignored all of us."

If he struggled with sports, he appeared to persevere. On May 18, 2001, a short blurb appeared in the *Newtown Bee*, the town's local weekly newspaper, after Adam's Little League team, Taunton Press, defeated Bob Tendler Real Estate 11–4. It described Adam's performance as "stellar in the field."

As he grew up, Adam seemed uninterested in forging any human relationships outside his immediate family. And even within the family home, the only person he felt truly comfortable around was his mother. He always wanted her near him but still managed to keep her at arm's length.

One night when Adam had a fever, Nancy slept on the floor all night outside his closed door. Periodically he would call out, "Are you there? Are you there?"

"Yes, I'm here," Nancy always responded.

The older Adam became, the more his unusual behavior made him a target for the class bullies, and as he approached middle school, Nancy told friends that Sandy Hook wasn't doing enough to stop the taunting.

"They picked on his quietness; they knew he wouldn't fight back," Nancy told Marvin during a phone conversation. "The poor kid was an easy target."

Adam sometimes came home from the third grade with bruises on his body, another sign his mother believed he was being picked on. When questioned, Adam withdrew.

"She once told me she was so upset that teachers weren't protecting him against bullies that she went with him like a bodyguard," Marvin said. "Nancy would do anything to protect her son. She spoke to the teachers and said, 'I'm going to be sitting in the back of the school' . . . I remember that Nancy went to his class and nothing would happen."

Nancy had a zero-tolerance policy toward violence of any type, not just concerning her son. While she felt at ease with a high-powered rifle aimed at a target for sport, the country girl was by nature a pacifist. After being told in March 1999 of an incident in New Hampshire involving a student attacking another with a nail, an outraged Nancy hinted at her growing frustration over Adam's troubles.

"I was shocked when I read about the nail incident. I agree . . . that kid [with the nail] should be expelled from school," she wrote in an email that month. "[Schools] go on and on about their great 'zero tolerance' regarding drugs and alcohol . . . but go ahead and let a kid attack another with a weapon!

"They will spend THOUSANDS of dollars on that child to keep an aide sitting with him . . . and then they say they don't have money for one hour a week of speech therapy for a smart, quiet child with a speech impairment. I am totally disgusted with that school!" she wrote, referring to Adam.

Adam's need for space extended to the school bus, where he would often sit in the back, usually alone. "He didn't sit with the other kids and didn't seem to have any friends," said Marsha Moskowitz, who drove Adam on the bus for three years. "He was quiet, a very shy and reserved kid," she said, noting that Adam "did little to reach out and make friends. I never saw him try."

Still, despite her many grievances, overall Nancy was pleased with her son's progress during his first few years at Sandy Hook Elementary, and everything appeared to be looking up. He sat with the general student body in the classroom and did well academically. Parent-teacher conferences were always uneventful, with Adam's teachers giving nothing but good reports, other than occasionally reversing letters.

At home she noticed that more time was passing between temper tantrums. His Aspergers and sensory perception disorder were being managed.

"It's been frustrating and it's been a battle," Nancy emailed a friend as the fourth-grade year wound to an end. "But overall I have to admit that Adam has been making quite a bit of progress. I'm not sure we could have received this level of attention back home."

Although awkward, socially backward, and occasionally picked on and bullied, his family would later remember Adam's time at Sandy Hook Elementary as "the best times of his life."

In January 2003, more changes came as Adam entered Newtown's Reed Intermediate School for fifth and sixth grades. Lanza and his classmates were the first fifth-graders to attend the intermediate school, moving from Sandy Hook Elementary midyear in 2003.

Again, Adam's odd behavior made the eleven-year-old stick out to classmates. "He was extremely introverted and didn't talk to anyone," recalled Dan Lynch, a former classmate. "He was really skittish, and anxious. He kept to himself and everyone left him alone."

In the fall of 2004, Adam entered seventh grade at Newtown Middle School, and for the first three marking periods, his performance on paper academically was great. He achieved mostly A grades and his teacher described him as having a "positive attitude" and being "fully engaged and respectful." He also earned an A in gym class and won the praise of his band teacher.

Middle school, however, would represent a turning point in his young life. While in elementary school, Adam rarely had to move from room to room, something he had always struggled with; now that he was entering middle school he was frequently required to change classes.

Classmates could see the terror on his face as he tried to navigate a hallway. "He always looked terrified as he walked down the hall. His shoulders would slump and he would cling to the wall," one classmate said. "I remember thinking that he walks like he expects someone to hit him."

That year, his inability to deal with sights, sounds, and textures started to become more acute. From the din of the lunch bell to the commotion of students rushing through the halls, everything around Adam had become a source of constant irritation. The struggles were spilling over to his home life, too, where the outbursts started to become more violent as Adam became increasingly resistant about going to school.

Nancy fought with the school to accommodate her son's condition. "This is torture for my son," she told one school official.

The school did little to appease the angry mother, at least as far as Nancy was concerned. In turn, Nancy had developed a reputation as "tightly wound," "demanding," and with a "flare for dramatics" among some of the staff.

In 2005, Nancy had become fed up with how the academic district was dealing, or not dealing, with her son's difficulties. She pulled him out Newtown Middle School in April 2005 and enrolled him at St. Rose of Lima, the Catholic school in Newtown. Nancy wasn't religious, but she thought the smaller class sizes would ensure that her son received the kind of personal attention he so desperately needed.

Still, Adam's troubles continued to escalate. He just could not fit in. While most children were talking about Avril Lavigne or the latest Harry Potter book, on the rare occasions when he did speak, it was often about fifties rock music or aliens.

"Adam had a difficult time making the adjustment from public school to St. Rose," said Monsignor Robert Weiss, the pastor of the parish. "He struggled."

More bad news came the Lanza family's way when a teacher discovered a collection of disturbing graphics Adam had drawn. The images depicted people in various states of death. The educator brought them to the attention of school officials, who felt the drawings warranted enough concern to bring Nancy in for a parent-teacher conference. She defensively told the faculty by way

of explanation that Adam had Asperger's syndrome and was struggling to fit in.

Adam's time at his new Catholic school lasted just eight weeks.
In June 2005, Nancy pulled him out of St. Rose of Lima. She was
increasingly at a loss about what to do next and becoming more
concerned. At home, she found more death-themed drawings by
Adam and images of violence that he had printed out from his computer. Again, desperately searching for help for her troubled son,
she consulted an expert in Hartford, Connecticut. Again, she didn't
feel that her concerns were being addressed.

"If one more person tells me that he is going to grow out of it, I
think I'm going to lose my mind," Nancy confided to a relative. "My
son is sick, but no one seems to want to do anything about it."

CHAPTER 4

⟨o⟩

THE HIGH SCHOOL YEARS

As Adam Lanza was about to enter his first year of high school in the fall of 2006, Nancy felt encouraged. Finally, she believed, she had found an advocate at Newtown High School who would be responsive to her son's needs and was willing to work with his Asperger's syndrome and sensory perception disorder.

"Very encouraged with Newtown High," Nancy wrote, sending a message to a friend. "Fingers crossed."

Nancy had been looking forward to the beginning of the school year. Over the summer her worries about her son's mental health were compounding. While the other children in Sandy Hook were busy swimming in the pool at Treadwell Memorial Park or cooling off with some homemade ice cream at the Ferris Acres Creamery, Adam continued to isolate himself, spending the vast majority of his summer vacation between the walls of 36 Yogananda Street on his computer or playing video games.

"It's so hard to pull him out of his own little world," Nancy told a friend that summer. "Still searching for that healthy balance of pushing him hard enough while not pushing him too hard."

Nancy hoped that a new academic year and a new school environment might snap her son out of his self-imposed solitude. Working with the Newtown High School administration and Richard J. Novia, the head of security, as well as the school's Tech Club adviser, they devised a program in which Adam would begin in a private classroom. This appealed to Nancy because it would mean Adam would be alone, where it would be quiet and he wouldn't have to move from room to room, which could set him off. In time, if all went well, Adam would then be folded back into the main building with a mix of special education and honors classes.

Adam joined the Tech Club, a group of forty students who created robots, built computers, and even ran their own TV show that filmed local sporting events. The instructor, Novia, agreed to take special precautions while Adam was around the equipment. Since Adam didn't feel physical pain like a normal person because of his sensory perception disorder, whenever Adam was using soldering tools and other potentially dangerous equipment he had to be closely watched.

From the beginning it was apparent to the class that Adam was a natural in the world of computers. As a sophomore in a class filled with juniors and seniors, he immediately stood out as the only one who could build a computer from scratch. His eyes grew wide and he seemed to go off into his own world as his hands and mind worked fluidly to wire complex circuitry onto the motherboard.

Novia, who started the Tech Club, saw Adam's potential and

fragility and immediately took the fourteen-year-old under his wing. He worked with him patiently, trying to get him to join the rest of the group.

"I wanted to help him," said Novia. "There was this glimmer in his eye and I believed that if we just tapped into that we could bring him out. He was brilliant. Most kids needed manuals and instructions to work the video editing. Adam didn't need any of that. He had a natural gift."

Novia met several times with Nancy Lanza to discuss Adam's problems. She told Novia that Adam suffered from Asperger's and sensory perception disorder. Adam had also been the victim of bullying, Nancy told Novia, and that faculty and administrators at his previous schools hadn't done enough to protect him.

"I promised her that Adam would be protected and that no one would lay a hand on Adam so long as I was at the school," said Novia.

It was clear right away that Adam would need close supervision.

"He fit the profile that suggested future problems, so we all kept an eye on him, right down to the custodians," said Novia.

Like his years in middle school, ninth grade proved to be a struggle for Adam. He remained introverted and continued to seek out isolation.

"He would withdraw and sit in the corner, or stand off by himself and wobble back and forth," said Novia. "He was constantly looking around. I never saw Adam laugh or smile. It was as if he was afraid of the world."

But after a few months Novia began to see modest signs of progress in his student. When instructed as to which camera to stand behind, Adam wouldn't verbally respond but, after he became familiar with the process, would comply.

"That was major progress," said Novia.

But as much as the instructor worked to bring him out of his shell, the awkward teen spent the majority of his time sitting alone inside the control room for video productions of the Tech Club's channel 17. He would stay inside for hours with the door closed. The only light in the room came from the glow of the computer screens and monitors.

If there had been some signs of a brief respite from his disorders, it wouldn't be long before Adam's struggle with mental illness started to cripple him again. Almost on a weekly basis, he began having episodes that sent him into complete withdrawal. Loud noises, bright lights, or any sudden change or excitement could send him into a nonresponsive state. These episodes seemed to come on at random. If the other students began to organize a game of capture the flag, Adam saw the excitement building and sought out a quiet spot in a corner to sit down by himself.

"It was like he would go into a trance," one student remembered. "It was a little scary. No one picked on him or anything. He just seemed vacant. Like he wasn't there."

The instructor sometimes sat next to him, patiently coaxing him back to reality. Adam rarely responded. The episodes sometimes ended with a call to Nancy, who immediately came to the school and soothingly touched her son's arm and rubbed his back before carefully escorting him to the car.

His special needs were also obvious to Latin teacher Jennifer Huettner. The nervous thirteen-year-old arrived each morning in

Huettner's private classroom wearing the same loose-fitting khaki pants and baggy blue polo shirt buttoned tightly at his neck. He carried a small pocket protector that contained pens, along with a black briefcase that he carried with him everywhere as his security blanket.

The briefcase was nearly empty, containing only a few personal notes and drawings.

"It was strange. This large briefcase filled with nothing but a few papers," said one person who was familiar with its contents. "He wrote a lot about his parents' separation. It bothered him greatly."

Before sitting down, the first thing Adam did was to make sure his desk was sanitary. He would take out a small bottle of Purell and carefully wipe every spot to make sure it was germ-free. It had been a habit Adam had picked up several years earlier when he first became fixated on germs, especially when it came to food. If he thought someone might have touched his meal, he refused to eat, no matter how hungry he may have been. Once Adam was convinced that every spot had been sanitized, he would deliberately pull his seat out, put his bag down, and sit.

Over time, Adam seemed to adapt to his new teacher and was a quick study with Latin. However, he was still uncomfortable and needed the assurance that his mother was nearby. Nancy obliged. She would wait in an empty room next door, reading a book while Adam had his lesson.

That was typical of Nancy, who continued to keep a close eye on Adam.

"It's hard to imagine a more devoted mother," said Novia. "She was so involved in her son's life. Sometimes I would say, 'Nancy, you need to go home. Leave him,' but it was hard for her to let him out of her sight."

At the beginning of his sophomore year, the decision was made to try to move Adam from the private classroom into the main high school building. At first Nancy was hesitant. The nightmarish experience of eighth grade only two years earlier was still fresh in her mind. She wasn't so sure her son was ready for all the noise and commotion that comes with joining a group of four hundred teenagers but, after receiving several assurances from the school staff that her son's needs would be accommodated, she decided to give it a try.

For the faculty, who always kept an eye out for incoming students requiring special attention, Adam's problems appeared more severe than most and they made sure they had protocols in place to handle his challenges. Among the fears now that Adam would be integrated into the main school was the reality that Adam could be an easy target for bullies. The school's three security staffers were told to monitor him carefully and to report where he was, who he was with, and what he was doing at all times to their higher-ups. Adam was also assigned a high school psychologist who would check in with him and Nancy periodically, while teachers and counselors were also informed of his heightened sensitivities. An escort was assigned to walk him through the hallways when needed, and many of the faculty had Nancy's number at their disposal if anything went wrong.

Nancy remained cynical, but was also encouraged. "The school couldn't be more helpful," Nancy wrote a friend. "There might still be hope yet."

On the first day of his sophomore year at Newtown High School, Adam made a fashion change, switching from the blue polo shirt he wore every day as a freshman to a green polo shirt. He would go on to wear it for the rest of the school year. In the class-room Adam's odd behavior caused him to stick out to classmates. Unlike most teen boys his age, Adam did everything he could to avoid drawing attention to himself. His anxiety became apparent whenever the teacher called on him to answer a question. Feeling the eyes of the class looking in his direction, he squirmed and struggled to get the words out, but when he finally did utter his response, the answer was always right.

Adam followed a careful routine when having to navigate the hallway. He always sat near the door so he could readily slip out after the bell rang or he waited in his seat until the crowds had cleared. Then, slightly hunched over and walking with his shoulder against the wall and holding his briefcase out to protect himself, he moved swiftly through the corridors toward the exit. He always took the same route, and never deviated from it. At Excel Tutoring in Newtown, where Adam sometimes went for extra classes, it was also obvious that he had trouble sitting still and couldn't stop fidgeting.

Adam did make one rare social connection during his sopho-more year, with classmate Alan Diaz, a freshman. The two played video games together, but Adam remained withdrawn and rarely spoke. Nancy invited Diaz and the Tech Club over to her house on one occasion in the hope that it might help her son engage with his peers. Adam appeared to enjoy himself as the group played *Star-Craft,* a war game set in space, and *Warcraft III.*

Despite Adam's continued troubles in adjusting, Novia continued to see small signs of progress. Adam began participating in an after-school program, helping to tape basketball games. He even let go of his briefcase, switching to a bag that carried his laptop.

"He felt safe. He started to come out of his shell," said Novia. "Nancy saw the progress, too. It was exciting to see."

As Adam finished his sophomore year he became increasingly interested in target shooting. Nancy, who continued to be concerned about his isolation, had been looking for any opportunity to connect with her son, especially in a way that would get him out of the house. The shooting range provided the perfect outlet.

"She'd take him to the range a lot. It was a way they could bond with each other," her former landscaper Dan Holmes said. "Nancy was an enthusiast and she wanted to pass her passion along to her kids."

The choice of this mother-son bonding pastime struck some as strange. When his old classmate Alan Diaz, who by then had lost touch with Adam, ran into Nancy and asked her how his friend was doing, he was surprised by the response.

"He's good. He started going to the shooting range with me," Nancy explained.

Adam? At the shooting range? Diaz thought. *That's weird. I never really imagined Adam as the type to hold a gun.*

On March 29, 2010, Nancy Lanza went into Riverview Gun

Sales in East Windsor, Connecticut, and purchased a Bushmaster XM15 rifle. A year later she purchased the SIG Sauer 9-millimeter pistol on March 16, 2011, at the same store. On the ATF 4473s, the firearms transaction forms that she was required by law to fill out, she checked the box yes on both forms to the question, "Are you the actual transferee/buyer of the firearm(s) listed on this form?"

The forms warn that if you are buying the firearm on behalf of another person, "the dealer cannot transfer the firearm(s) to you," and that it is a federal crime to give a false answer. She checked the box for no on both forms to the question, "Have you ever been adjudicated mentally defective (which includes a determination by a court, board, commission, or other lawful authority that you are a danger to yourself or to others or are incompetent to manage your own affairs) OR have you ever been committed to a mental institution?"

Some of the weapons Nancy bought she kept. Others she gave to Adam.

Besides the gun range, the only other place Adam traveled to was the local video game store, GameStop, where he would enter, get what he needed, and leave. But it was within the safe confines of his home that Nancy could see her son's behavior really changing. Adam's frequent bouts of panic and tantrums kept getting worse. He was acting oddly, making more strange drawings, and had begun muttering to himself.

Overall, Adam's struggles in social interactions continued to be apparent to everyone who crossed his path. Even a haircut proved a harrowing experience. Every few months the routine played out.

Nancy walked in, with Adam following closely behind, and instructed Adam as to where exactly to sit. As he was cutting his hair, Bob Skuba, the stylist, tried every trick in his book to get the teenager to laugh or acknowledge him, but always failed.

"I'd always make jokes and try to talk to him but he looked at me like I was invisible. He just wouldn't say a word," Skuba recalled. "Adam would stare down at the tiles. He would never make eye contact."

At the end of the haircut, Skuba would say, "You're all set, Adam." But he wouldn't get out of his chair—not "until the mother came over and grabbed him by the arm and would say, 'All right, you are done. You can go now, Adam.' The only time he moved or made any kind of response in any way was when his mother told him to," Skuba said.

Without saying a word, Adam would walk straight out the door with his mother in close pursuit. "It was obvious that he was different. Something was wrong with him."

Adam's older brother, Ryan, obviously noticed the severity of his brother's differences but dismissed them more nonchalantly. "My brother has always been a nerd," he explained when he was once asked what was wrong with his younger brother.

But just as it appeared Adam was beginning to slowly adjust to the routine at Newtown High School, right before beginning his junior year, Nancy learned that Richard Novia would be leaving the school. Wary of the rest of the Newtown administration and faculty, Nancy knew the only person she could trust to look out for her troubled son was leaving and decided to take Adam out of the school.

Novia heard the news and pleaded with Nancy to keep Adam in school, believing that removing him could "send him in a tailspin."

"I told her that Adam was making progress and that taking him out of school could send him in reverse. He had a support network. Without the school, he would fall back into isolation. He would lose all of his interactions. Everything would be stripped from him. He would get worse."

Nancy wouldn't budge. "If you are not going to be there, I'm taking him out," Nancy told Novia in a phone call. "I don't trust anyone else." Her intense anger at and distrust of the school overwhelmed any arguments to the contrary and she insisted that Adam be taken out.

"She didn't trust anyone else. She had a lot of anger at the school administration. She was very unhappy with the entire district," said Novia. "Nancy didn't believe Adam would get the attention he needed without me there."

Novia also noted: "There was just no pleasing Nancy. She wanted Adam watched one hundred percent of the time. She wanted every faculty member to be just as dedicated to her son as she was. She directed her anger at the special ed teacher, the guidance counselor, the administration."

The school had failed her son, Nancy believed. Adam was angry with the school, too. With no social life or friends, school was all he had and now that was gone.

Nancy pulled her son out of Newtown High School after his junior year and enrolled him at Western Connecticut State University, hoping that Adam would thrive in a more adult environment where there would be less chaos. After passing his GED test in the summer of 2008, he took a total of seven classes and earned a 3.26 GPA his first year. He took Website Production, Visual Basic, Data Modeling, American History since 1877, and Introduction to Ethical Theory, a course in which he got a C.

But signs of his mental instability were always present. When asked on his college application to indicate a gender, Adam wrote: "I choose not to answer," followed by the question, "How do you describe yourself?" Even his university ID photo—his brown eyes bulging, his face seemingly devoid of emotion—suggested to some that something about him was off.

Adam always sat alone, toward the back of the class, often wearing a hooded sweatshirt. He never spoke. At Western Connecticut State University, Adam, who was several years younger than his classmates, again didn't fit in. If a classmate greeted him, Adam acted nervous and avoided eye contact. After an Introduction to German class in spring 2009, two girls asked Adam if he wanted to join them for a drink.

"No, I can't. I'm seventeen," he responded.

Still, Nancy had hopes that her son would excel in a more adult environment and didn't entertain the possibility of enrolling him back at Newtown High School. "Newtown [school] is dead to me," she told a friend.

Dealing with her son's condition wasn't the only issue Nancy had to deal with domestically. Her marriage, which had been acrimonious for years, was finally over. On September 23, 2009, she and Peter finalized their divorce. Whatever their marital problems, the divorce was by all accounts amicable, the main concern of both being the welfare of Adam. The couple agreed that Adam, then sixteen, would live primarily with his mother, but that his father would have "liberal visitation and vacations." True to his word, Peter continued to see his sons weekly, taking them skiing, hiking, rock climbing, to coin shows, and on overnight stays at his Stamford apartment until 2010, when Adam broke off contact with his father after Peter began seriously dating again. He also severed ties with his brother, Ryan, and his uncle James, whom he had been close to as a child.

The agreement also meant that Nancy would be financially taken care of for the rest of her life, which worked to the family's advantage—both Nancy and Peter knew that she could never take on a full-time job and still care for their son. At the time of their divorce, Peter earned $8,556 a week. In 2010, he agreed to pay an annual alimony of $240,000, with increases each year. By 2012, he was paying $289,000, and after 2016, Nancy would receive an annual cost-of-living increase based on the 2015 alimony payment of $298,000 per year until he retired.

Peter and Nancy were also required to attend a parenting-education program, a standard practice in Connecticut. Both parents successfully completed the required sessions. In working through the terms of their divorce, they spent a considerable amount of time talking about how to provide for Adam's well-being, said Paula Levy, a mediator who worked with the couple. During their meetings, Paula said they appeared to be on the same page regarding how to best address his needs.

"The mom, Nancy, pretty much said she was going to take care of him and be there as much as he needed her, even long term. She was very concerned about Adam, [but] both parents were very attentive to his needs. The [one] thing I remember them saying is that they really don't like leaving him alone," Paula said.

According to the divorce settlement approved by Judge Stanley Novak, Nancy would have the final say concerning any aspect of Adam's upbringing. Peter agreed to pay the entire cost of his sons' college and graduate school educations, and also agreed to purchase a car for Adam. Nancy was to cover the car insurance and cost of maintenance. The now divorced couple also agreed to divide their season Red Sox tickets; Nancy would get two tickets for five games in odd years and four games in even years. Peter moved to the affluent Stamford suburb of Westover and the family home at 36 Yogananda Street went to Nancy, who was to live there with Adam, as Ryan had gone off to college.

Then in 2010, Peter remarried. His second wife was Shelley Cudiner, a reference librarian and business liaison at the University of Connecticut's Jeremy Richard Library. Nancy occasionally dated, but remained largely unattached. She was an independent woman who throughout her life had become accustomed to taking care of herself and depending on no one else. "Who has time for a serious relationship?" she'd said to a friend recently. "Besides, I have to be there for Adam. You always have to be there for your kids."

Meanwhile, Adam's time was becoming increasingly consumed by his computer, where his mother noticed him researching weapons, wars, and the military. "He's fixated on becoming a marine," Nancy told a friend, knowing that it could never happen.

She had tried a new specialist in Danbury in hopes of helping Adam, but again was let down. Still, Nancy kept holding out hope that a turnaround for her youngest son was just around the corner. "He's too brilliant not to eventually succeed," she told relatives.

CHAPTER 5

---◄○►---

ENTER KAYNBRED

The abrupt end of Adam Lanza's high school career correlated with a new online persona, an alias he created named "Kaynbred" that began to reveal his growing fixation with violence.

Beginning in 2009, at the age of seventeen, Adam created this new fictitious user name and began frequenting Internet chat rooms that focused on violent video games, weapons, and, most disturbing of all, mass killers. Alone and in the darkness, with the illuminated screen his only light, Adam had found a level of comfort in his world of computers and video games that he could rarely attain in the outside world. Behind "Kaynbred," Adam was able to show a bravado and confidence that was unfamiliar to classmates and family who only knew him as an awkward and meek teenager.

The first signs of this abnormal obsession became evident at age fifteen, when Adam delved into *World of Warcraft*, a game in which players live in an alternate universe of dragons and monsters and must heroically conquer darkness and competitors to move ahead. By September 2009, Adam had become a regular fixture in the online gaming community for *Combat Arms*, a multiplayer first-person shooting game where the player is in control of a gun. The object of the game, like most first-person shooter games, is to kill the most enemy players. In Adam's chosen "mission," gamers had to achieve a set number of kills. The team that reached the most kills in the quickest amount of time was the winner, even if that meant turning the gun on yourself and committing suicide.

He was quickly accepted into the group of other online players as part of a "cluster," who discussed strategies and gaming obstacles mixed in with small talk and occasional jokes. His online interactions went smoothly. He fit in and appeared well liked by the other players, showing none of the discomfort or struggle he would exhibit in face-to-face encounters.

Along with being a rare positive social experience for Adam, the game also provided an outlet for him to live out his growing military obsessions. In *Combat Arms*, Adam was allowed to create his own soldier, deciding everything from the clothes he wore and the weapons he used to the backdrop for the battles he fought.

In his alternative online universe, the skinny and frail teenager chose to create an imposing bulky muscle-bound soldier dressed in desert camouflage and also a light vest, goggles, and a black beret. He chose equally imposing weapons for his missions: the M16A3, a military variant of the Bushmaster AR-15 assault rifle, and the G23 pistol, which strongly resembles a Glock 10-millimeter handgun. Adam's battlefield of choice was called the "Death Room," a seemingly abandoned secret facility with a multitude of tightly spaced areas.

Adam quickly immersed himself in this virtual world, logging thousands of kills over hundreds of hours of playing time. His *Combat Arms* online profile showed he played 4,901 matches or games, clocking more than 500 hours in front of the screen and tallying 83,496 kills, including 22,725 "head shots."

While many opponents in Adam's online cluster bragged about cheating by using codes that gave them an advantage over other players, Adam was "clean," according to a watchdog group that monitored cheaters. He did not need to dupe the system to win.

That year Adam also joined an online community to indulge in another one of his passions: weapons. On August 25, 2009, Adam joined the gun-enthusiasts message board at thehighroad.com, a Website that bills itself as a group where "responsible gun ownership is discussed, threads include firearms specifications, tools and technology with Activism and rally points."

While Adam kept his posts to a minimum, focusing mostly on legalities and questions about how to convert semiautomatic guns into automatic weapons, the seventeen-year-old's brazen online persona displayed a vast knowledge of firearms. He easily kept pace with the group of primarily older adults.

From his first entry, it was already clear that he was well versed in weaponry when he opened up a discussion comparing two types of rifles:

"The CZ Vz. 58 is a rifle which is similar to the AK-47 only through their shared 7.62x39mm caliber and aesthetics. It functions entirely differently and has no interchangeable parts with the AK-47, including the magazine."

Adam then listed the Connecticut gun laws:

"My state (Connecticut) has its own state-level assault weapons ban. In it is the following: Sec. 53-202a. Assault weapons: Definition. (a) . . . inclusive, "assault weapon" means: (1) . . . any of the following specified semiautomatic firearms: . . . Avtomat Kalashnikov AK-47 type . . .

"According to what I have read, to be an 'AK-47 type', the firearm must be aesthetically similar to an AK-47, operate similarly, and have interchangeable parts. From a perfunctory search of Google, I have seen multiple people claim that because the CZ Vz. 58 does not meet these three requirements, it is not an 'AK-47 type' and it is thus legal for sale in Connecticut. Does anyone have any information on this?"

Two responses were posted on the board: "It's not an AK type at all. Enjoy your Vz58:)," one responded.

"It's not an AK-47 type. Just make sure you get one with a fixed stock so that it conforms to the other stupid part of the CT AWB," responded another.

Adam posted appreciatively early the next morning at 1:42 A.M.: "I suppose that if a PTR-91 (almost an exact clone of an HK-91) is allowed, then a Vz. 58 would be. Thank you.:)"

In another thread, started on August 27, 2009, Adam posted another question about the legality of modifying a firearm so that it can shoot more bullets more quickly:

"In Connecticut, fully automatic firearms are legal to own but selective fire is prohibited. I vaguely recall reading ~1 year ago about a company which alters them to fire exclusively automatically (or something in that vein), but I do not know how that process works. For example, with whom would I correspond to modify a Title II M2 Carbine that is currently in another state to fire fully automatically before it is sent to Connecticut?"

Several members on the message board responded with suggestions.

Later that day, Adam responded to a post from a member looking for suggestions on what kind of weapon to purchase for himself for his birthday:

"Have you looked at the Kel-Tec SU-16? It can be found for under $650 and utilizes STANAG magazines."

Besides showing off his encyclopedic knowledge of weaponry, his posts also revealed his discomfort with face-to-face interactions. On October 12, 2009, he began a discussion titled "The legality of the CZ vz. 61 Skorpion in CT?" and asked: "A pistol referred to as the 'Scarab Skorpion' is banned. Does anyone know if that by extension bans the unrelated CZ vz. 61?"

After one person suggested that Adam contact the Connecticut State Police, he responded by writing that he preferred not to deal with anyone in person. "I always prefer asking through proxy when I can avoid speaking to someone directly. I was just wondering if anyone knew because I have a fetish for .32 ACP," he replied the next day.

In one post, on October 13, 2009, Adam even showed a sense of humor when posting on another weapons discussion board, Glock Talk: "Am I just an inattentive philistine or has additional RAM in a computer which was not already deprived of it never helped any of you?"

. . .

As Adam's mastery of violent video games and high-powered weapons developed, another fixation began to reveal itself. Between August 2009 and February 2010, Adam spent hours poring over entries about mass killers on Wikipedia. Still under the alias "Kaynbred," Adam went into the communal encyclopedia, obsessively correcting small details of the killers' lives.

One entry Adam worked on was the Collier Township shooting where, on August 4, 2009, George Sodini walked into a health club in a suburb of Pittsburgh, and killed three and injured nine before taking his own life. In another posting Adam revised the description of a firearm used in the September 13, 2006, shooting at Dawson College in Montreal. In that incident, gunman Kimveer Gill began shooting outside the main entrance of the school, killing one and injuring nineteen others before shooting himself in the head. Adam posted about the weapon used in the deadly attack: "A '9mm' was listed as '.9mm'. People say that 9mm is anemic, but this is ridiculous."

Adam also edited details of the Westroads Mall shooting where, on December 5, 2007, gunman Robert Hawkins walked into the Von Maur department store in Omaha, Nebraska, and shot twelve people, killing four, before turning the gun on himself. Adam then diverted his attention to the entry about the "Luby massacre" in Killeen, Texas. On October 16, 1991, George Hennard crashed his pickup truck through the front window of a Luby's cafeteria, shot fifty people, killing twenty-three, then hid in a bathroom and fatally shot himself before police arrived.

Adam also made minor edits on the Wikipedia post for Larry Gene Ashbrook, who opened fire on a teen prayer rally at the Wedgwood Baptist Church in Fort Worth, Texas, killing seven teenagers and injuring seven others on September 15, 1999. Ashbrook also committed suicide. The list went on. In an article on mass killer Kip Kinkel, Adam corrected details about the weapons used in the slaying. Kinkel was a teenager when he murdered his parents in their Springfield, Oregon, home on May 20, 1998. The next day he headed to Thurston High School and killed two students and wounded twenty-five others before being apprehended by police.

The original post listed the weapons as a "9 mm Glock pistol, a Sturm, Ruger .22 semi-automatic rifle, and a Ruger .22 pistol." Adam corrected the post to read: "9 mm Glock pistol, sawn-off .22LR, Ruger 10/22 rifle, .22LR, Ruger MK II."

Other mass killers Adam studied included:

• Ibrahim Shkupolli, who committed the Sello mall shooting in Finland on New Year's Eve 2009. Shkupolli killed his ex-girlfriend and four workers at a shopping center before turning the gun on himself.

• Robert Ryan, who on August 19, 1987, killed sixteen people, including his mother, and wounded fifteen others before fatally shooting himself in the so-called Hungerford massacre.

• Richard Farley, who on February 16, 1988, killed seven and wounded four others at his former place of employment in Sunnyvale, California, before being apprehended by law enforcement.

Two other message boards Adam joined but never posted on were "Northeasternshooters forum," another board for gun enthusiasts, and "Veggie Boards," a message board for vegetarians. In February 2010 the posts abruptly stopped.

Adam received his driver's license in 2010 but he rarely took out the car. Occasionally he headed to the gun range or drove the four miles to the nearby video game store, but these excursions decreased in frequency over time. He also enrolled in Norwalk Community College in the fall of 2010 but soon dropped out. With his academic career over, there was even less real need to leave his house. He began increasing the amount of time he spent playing video games.

By 2011, Adam had stopped playing Combat Arms and moved on to *Call of Duty* and *Call of Duty: Modern Warfare 2*, both violent, first-person shooting games where, like Combat Arms, players compete to rack up the most number of "kills." In *Call of Duty: Modern Warfare 2*, the atrocities of combat are re-created by putting the players in the middle of a civilian slaughter. With his hand on the controller, Adam became an undercover CIA agent who joined a group of Russian terrorists at an airport to massacre unarmed civilians. To keep his cover and fulfill the mission's objective, he had to shoot and kill women and children. The injured would crawl away leaving a smeary trail of blood, while those spared from the spray made the futile attempt to help others only to be shot dead.

Adam became an expert, able to navigate through the different war zones, killing everything in his path with relative ease. Moving from scene to scene, the skill of quickly reloading before his magazine emptied was vital to acquiring the most kills in the shortest amount of time. Through repetitive play of *Call of Duty*, Adam learned how to load the second cartridge in a single fluid motion before the first was emptied by ejecting the magazine with the hand holding the weapon while drawing a new magazine from its place using his fourth and fifth fingers, and inserting a fresh magazine with the thumb and index finger. That skill, called the "tactical reload," had previously been available only to law enforcement or for military training.

Call of Duty allowed him to try different techniques with a wide variety of weapons. He could choose pistols, automatic weapons, and even flamethrowers to execute his mission. After much trial and error, he settled on the AN-94 as his favorite, a fully automatic Russian assault rifle that could cause maximum damage, especially in short bursts.

By 2012, Adam had slipped into further solitude. "It was nearly complete isolation and it was self-imposed," one relative recalled. "Adam was by himself all the time and there was nothing Nancy or anyone else could do to get him out. She tried, but he just wouldn't have it. The more she tried, the more she believed she pushed him further and further away."

Another friend referred to Adam as a "shut-in." His mental health issues, combined with his military ambitions, his gaming habit, and a dramatic decline in any form of social interaction had caused the young man to withdraw further and further from reality. Even the shooting range was barely appealing.

CHAPTER 6

WARNING SIGNS

Nancy, too, began to change. She had always been an attractive, upbeat blonde known for her unique brand of humor and sarcasm. But friends noticed that she was spending more and more time away from home and started talking about "getting away." In the fall, in anticipation of the move, she parted with one of her most prized possessions—her beloved Red Sox season tickets.

Neighbors began to notice a shift toward seclusion in the Lanza family. Their sprawling yellow Colonial family home, hidden away in a wooded area at the end of Yogananda Street, had been so full of life during its first few years but had since became a "black spot" in the neighborhood. The family had earned a reputation as very quiet, private, and largely unknown.

"I knew every single one of my neighbors but them," recalled one neighbor who lived three houses down. "Hardly anyone spoke to them. It's as if they stopped being part of the community altogether and just fell off the face of the earth."

Although Nancy had dedicated so much of her life and energy to helping her son, she sensed that her ability to keep a handle on the situation was slipping from her grasp. Her child was well past a point of crisis and, whatever was going on inside his head at this point, was beyond her ability to comprehend.

"Parental bonds are formed so early in life . . . they are either there or they aren't," she had emailed a friend more than a decade earlier, during an easier time when she still felt optimistic about her ability to shape Adam's future. "It is a direct product of how much the parent put into that relationship."

Now, her attitude had shifted. With Adam, perhaps it was already too late, she confided in a friend. Nancy was becoming accustomed to leaving her son alone for days, sometimes weeks at a time. Beginning in January 2012, she traveled to London, New Orleans, and New York City, in addition to frequent trips to Boston.

On October 6, 2012, Nancy emailed a relative about her extensive travels and plans to eventually downsize her home. She was waiting for the market to improve before listing the Yogananda Street residence with a Realtor.

"I hear you there . . . no sense selling at a loss!" she wrote. "Best to keep stability in the kids' lives. Moves are so tough at that age. I am still in the same place but getting to the point where I may want a smaller house. I travel a lot (a little bit of everywhere . . . Boston, New York, Maine, Toronto, London, San Francisco, Nantucket, Charlotte, Baltimore . . . that covers this year) spend time with friends, work with a couple of charities. Low key life and very happy."

Nancy spent Thanksgiving 2012 in northern New England with family, leaving Adam home alone with a prepared meal in the fridge. She had come to realize that she could not let her own life come to a grinding halt because of her son. His social interactions had dwindled to rare trips to the shooting range—getting him to a holiday feast with relatives was out of the question.

She told friends she planned on being out of town for Christmas, too, but didn't say where. These long stretches away from home didn't seem to worry her though. She somehow thought her absence might make Adam more independent. When a close friend asked if she was concerned about her son spending so much time alone, Nancy said she wasn't worried. Adam needed more solitary time than most people.

"He's fine," she said reassuringly. "Just so long as he has his computer and his video games, he can keep himself occupied."

In 2012, Nancy Lanza also learned that her father had a secret life in Ohio and that she had a half sister she had previously not known about. On October 6, 2012, she emailed her sister-in-law Marsha Lanza about recently reconnecting with a long-lost family member, Cheryl.

"I discovered I have a half sister in Ohio, so I have to get there to meet her soon!"

"Ha! Yes, indeed . . . definitely part gypsy."

"Yah . . . that's what I thought too but apparently my father was married previously and actually lived in Ohio . . . secret life and all. Weird. Cincinnati . . . Story TOO long to text off my little I Phone . . . But yes, life is funny and strange.

"Lies people tell and try to live in those lies. Sad. She seems nice and I would like to meet her. I feel sorry that my parents turned their backs on her at such a young age. No one is talking so I don't know the real story.

"As for Cheryl . . . she had no clue what happened. Her mother is dead, our father is dead, and my mother won't say. It's a mystery. We will never have answers . . . just have to deal with what is.

"Ryan works in Manhattan . . . Adam still at home. Yes, they do grow up too fast. I am off to bed . . . SO good to hear from you. Let's keep in touch! Maybe I can visit you when I visit my sister . . . I'll be halfway there."

The last communication from Marsha to Nancy came on December 14, 2012, when she sent one last message that was never returned. "Hi Nancy, Just checking in to see if you are OK and what you might know about the school shooting. Isn't this the town you live in? not sure. Drop me a line when you get a chance. My prayers go out to all."

The second week of December 2012, Nancy dropped by My Place Pizza & Restaurant, and Dennis Durant greeted her with a beer and chatted with her for half an hour or so, as they did two to three days a week. She was her usual bubbly self; there wasn't the slightest indication that anything could be wrong until halfway through her third draft.

"I don't know what else I can do for him," she confided to Durant. "I'm running out of answers."

Nancy did not have to say "his" name. Adam was sick and getting sicker. Her twenty-year-old son had been acting out more over the past few months, throwing temper tantrums triggered by the mere mention of the future. Any break from his routine made him hysterical. He would often stomp and scream, and then not speak to her for days.

Over the years Nancy had grown to accept such episodes. She could deal with temper tantrums. But as she sipped her beer, she told Durant it was the severe bouts of isolation coupled with a growing obsession with the military that had her worried.

As a kid, Adam hoped to follow in the footsteps of his uncle James, a Green Beret, and join the military. He admired his uncle, often telling family members when he was little, "I'm going to be just like Uncle Jim." At first Nancy encouraged Adam's desire to follow in his uncle's footsteps, thinking the discipline of the armed forces would give him structure and help channel his nervous energy. Yet she soon realized that the deteriorating state of his mental health would adversely affect his future plans.

Nancy had always looked up to her brother, too. "I don't know if there is a name for the kind of training the Green Berets get . . . they are simply trained to kill," Nancy emailed a friend back in the late 1990s. "He taught me two moves that even someone my size can use . . . although I have never had the chance to test them, I am sure they are effective."

Nancy had been the victim of a physical assault in the early

1980s on the Boston Common and the incident had shaken her to her core. The physical confrontation happened in broad daylight and in front of onlookers and she had feared her attacker would follow her back to Kingston and victimize her again at home.

"Nancy was nervous about that. She felt that her life was in danger," an official from the Kingston Police Department recalled.

While the self-defense lessons from her brother were helpful, in another email she wrote, "I really miss having my brother right next to me. I always felt so safe that way. No one messes with you if your brother is a cop . . . I never fully appreciated how wonderful that was." As much as Nancy enjoyed her firearms for recreational use, without her brother around they also gave her a much-needed sense of security. Over the years she amassed an impressive collection of weaponry, including eleven knives, a starter pistol, a bayonet, three samurai swords, several firearms, and more than 1,600 rounds of ammunition.

Adam had at least four of his own guns that he'd picked out himself after researching them online and that he kept in a safe in his bedroom upstairs. Nancy told Durant that she exposed him to the firearms as a way to help him learn responsibility. Durant later said she shouldered the blame for her son's obsession. Target shooting and their mutual love of firearms had given her a way to connect with her children, especially Adam.

Nancy recalled a conversation she'd had with her son just a few weeks earlier when telling Durant about Adam's medical conditions crushing his dream of joining the armed forces: "I told Adam, in as gentle terms as possible, that he will never be a marine, that he's just not cut out for it and that life has something different planned for him. How can you be a marine if you won't let people touch you?"

But Adam took the news harder than even his mother expected. Instead of exploring other options for his future, he became more and more obsessed with the military. The basement, which Nancy had remodeled into a game room for Adam, now looked more like a military compound. Nearly every inch of the Sheetrock walls were covered with posters of weaponry and old tanks from World War II. Pictures of submarines, military equipment, and depictions of battle were proudly displayed.

In another room of the house, which she had originally designated as a space for exercise, Adam, often dressed from head to toe in military garb, had created an indoor shooting range where he used his pellet gun to shoot at paper and cardboard targets he had set up on a clothesline.

Nancy also told Durant about Adam's other obsession with violent video games. He would sit in front of the screen for hours, "zoned out," she explained. On the rare occasion that she watched him play, Nancy said she found the images downright disturbing. She told Durant she had begun to notice that lately her son rarely ventured outside his compound. "He's like a zombie in front of the screen," she said, noting that Adam sometimes sat playing the game well into the night and slept most of the day. He had no friends, and now, no future ambitions. His life revolved increasingly around the game of war.

He owned a Sony PlayStation 2, an X-Box 360, and hundreds of games, most of them war games that he had meticulously lined up in alphabetical order against his wall. He spent his waking hours acting out fantasies he learned from the violent video games. Nancy told Durant she was baffled by her normally restless son's unwavering focus on the screen.

Still, she noticed that the increasing amount of time Adam spent playing violent video games coincided with his growing aversion for affection. He had always hated human touch, but Nancy had been the exception. Now when she reached for him, Adam physically recoiled. Nancy was worried and wanted answers. She had recently decided to take a peek inside his upstairs bedroom.

After a few minutes of searching, she found a disturbing number of drawings stashed underneath Adam's nightstand. Most were pictures of guns, "normal teenage boy crap," she called it. But other sketches were gruesome depictions of death, images of mutilated corpses. One drawing she described was of a bloodied woman clutching a rosary as bullets ripped through her spine. Another sketch depicted a large rolling grassy field lined with the corpses of young children. In the drawing, the faces of the children were severely mutilated and couldn't be recognized. One sketch appeared to be a self-portrait of a younger Adam with blood gushing from a large hole in his forehead and his arms stretched upward to the sky in a posture of triumph.

Adam had found several more graphic images online, printed them out, and kept them in a manila folder. Like his sketches, most depicted death.

One of the pictures showed a gunman dressed all in black taking aim at a man on his knees. The man appeared to be begging for his life in the clearing of a forest with the gunman's rifle pointed at his head. The two were surrounded by dozens of dead bodies covered in blood.

The picture that disturbed Nancy the most showed a naked woman covered in transparent plastic wrap. Her hands were bound behind her back and her face had been contorted to give her the appearance of a smile. Lipstick had been sloppily painted on her face.

"It gives me the chills to even think about it," she told Durant.

Nancy had always respected her son's space and she felt conflicted about going through his personal belongings but was horrified by the discovery. Durant said she decided it was best for the time being not to approach Adam about the images. She feared he might further shut her out if he discovered this breach of his space.

"That would be it. He would never get over it if he knew I went through his things," she told Durant. "He would be lost forever."

Nancy expressed hope that a change of scenery might help him. She told friends she was preparing to move with Adam to Washington state and had already started looking into colleges in the Northwest. Perhaps he could channel his passion for the armed forces into a degree in military history, she said. At first Adam seemed receptive, even scrolling through online college catalogs with her. But in the last few days he had become unresponsive to the idea and had "shut down."

She had researched his condition and read several books in the hope of understanding how to help. Switching doctors, medications, and his schools had all failed. Nancy now felt as if she was running out of options.

"It's as if he's stuck so far deep down inside himself that he has lost touch with the world," she explained. "I'm worried I've lost him."

Her cell phone rang. Nancy excused herself to take the call. Durant overheard her rambling on to a friend about an upcoming antiques show. No, she would not be going; she would be out of town. The conversation had lasted less than ten minutes before she casually put her phone away and returned to the table. Then, just like that, Nancy Lanza was back to her normal, bubbly self. She smiled reassuringly. "Sorry to be a buzz kill. I'm sure everything will be fine. Really."

Durant tried to reassure Nancy that everything with Adam would be all right. It was no use. Nancy wasn't looking for advice. She just wanted to vent. He sensed that there was more she wanted to say, but he thought, *Another time.* She looked exhausted. Tonight was not the night.

The stress over Adam's increasingly odd behavior had evidently been taking its toll on Nancy's physical health. She was suffering from debilitating migraines, throbbing joint pain, and insomnia from the incessant worrying. Before she left My Place that evening, she confided in Durant that Adam wasn't the only one who was sick. Nancy had recently found out that she had an incurable autoimmune disease and if she didn't find a way to relax, her health would wane. He was taken aback. At the age of fifty-two, Nancy appeared the perfect picture of health.

Before parting ways in the parking lot that night, Nancy mentioned to Durant that she had booked two nights at a luxury spa resort in Bretton Woods, New Hampshire. She said she needed the rest. "I'll be back Wednesday night sometime," Nancy said as she walked toward her car. "Let's talk Thursday."

• • •

"I need a change of scenery, I think we both do," Nancy texted a friend on December 10, 2012, right before her trip to the spa, referring to herself and Adam. "We can all use a good cleansing of mind and soul from time to time!"

This change of scenery would be Nancy's second trip away from home in the past month, and her fourteenth that year. She had tried to get Adam to join her on these getaways before, but it was always a struggle. So she was not surprised when he turned down yet another opportunity to leave town.

When asked earlier that year by a friend if her son would be going with her when she went to New Orleans to see a concert, "No," she replied, "Adam doesn't like to go anywhere."

Eventually, Nancy stopped asking. But she desperately needed the steady stream of vacations for her own sanity and well-being. Not only that, but she was concerned about how much time she had left before her illness would limit her mobility. Nancy believed she had multiple sclerosis.

Nancy first noticed symptoms of MS in the late 1990s. In an email thread dating back to late 1999, she first revealed her grave health fears to a friend: "I am carrying the gene for this type of self-destruct," she wrote. "My diagnosis was not good. I was going under the premise that I had a limited time left . . . about enough to get the boys settled in . . . At one point I was trying to deal with the time frame of about 12 months."

In another email from the same time period, she wrote: "They found another lesion on my brain. I just spent the last two weeks having tests . . . some excruciatingly painful. Any hope I had that things were going to be OK or that I could be in any kind of a permanent remission are gone. There is this mad scurry to find out if anything can be done. I look at my boys and think about what will happen to them. I have put on this big brave face to my family, but I am terrified."

But the diagnosis hardly seemed to slow Nancy down. She appeared to be full of energy and rarely complained about her health. Most of her friends and family continued to believe she was the picture of health.

But in December 2012, she wrote another dramatic email about her deteriorating health to a close friend: "I've been living with a ticking time bomb inside of me for several years now and I fear it is about to go off. My grandfather suffered from the same condition. It wasn't pretty. It comes on very sudden and when it does there is nothing left to do."

MS was taking its toll on Nancy's body as much as Adam's condition was taking a toll on her mind. She hoped a few days' respite at the luxury Omni Mount Washington Resort would provide precisely the temporary relief she needed before Christmas. She checked into the New Hampshire hotel on Tuesday, December 11, at 12:10 P.M. and headed straight for the 25,000-square-foot spa room, purchasing a $450 deluxe package that included a manicure, a fifty-minute facial, a fifty-minute body treatment, and a fifty-minute massage.

Between the scent of aromatic candles and the scenic views of the White Mountain National Forest, Nancy finally found some peace. When a friend inquired as to how her trip was going, she messaged back with one word: "heavenly."

After spending the day in the spa, Nancy ate dinner in the hotel's restaurant with its menu chockful of New England "farm to plate specialties." Clearly enjoying her brief getaway, she sent a message to a friend on Facebook from the restaurant, describing the finely dressed tattooed couple sitting nearby.

"A shimmery evening dress looks less formal with daggers and skulls poking out," Nancy quipped, always one to invoke a bit of humor when the opportunity presented itself.

"Be forewarned," she added. "Tattoo girl has talked me into a dragon tattoo."

Later that night she called home to check on Adam. As she expected, he did not answer. She probably figured he was in the basement playing video games as usual. When he was gaming, Adam was in his own world and wouldn't pick up the phone, answer the door, or even take his eyes off the screen in front of him.

It didn't matter. She would be home the next day.

At 12:27 P.M. on Thursday, December 13, Nancy checked out of the Omni and began the five-hour trek back to Newtown. Normally she arrived home from trips to find the house virtually unchanged. Rarely was there even a dirty plate in the sink. The only real sign of life in the house would be a pile of soiled clothes in the hamper.

"Adam is like a ghost," she once told Durant. "He doesn't even leave footprints."

In a message to a friend in September 2012, Nancy had mentioned an ominous dream that now reads like more of a premonition. It began with her outside with her son enjoying a flawless blue-sky day when suddenly the clouds grew dark and a large gust of wind began lifting Adam up into the sky.

"All of a sudden he was being lifted up into the air and I was grabbing on to his ankles with both hands trying to keep him connected to the ground, but the harder I pulled the harder the wind kept blowing him away from me," she wrote. "Suddenly I couldn't hold on anymore and he lifted up into the sky. I stood there helplessly and watched as he got smaller and smaller."

She felt hopeless. Her whole life, Nancy had always felt the pressure to protect her son against the world, but in recent months her life's work, raising her son, felt like a lost cause.

"Sometimes I feel like I'm the only thing that anchors him to reality and without me he would be gone, gone gone."

CHAPTER 7

———◁◌▷———

THE PUBLIC SERVANTS

It was a typical Friday morning on Primrose Street. As December 14 kicked into gear, the smell of coffee wafted through the spacious hallways of the Newtown Town Hall and the offices bustled with the sound of small-town government hard at work.

Situated in a large majestic building that was formerly Bridgeport Hall, part of Fairfield Hills State Hospital, the town hall had become a one-stop gathering place for locals to pay bills, apply for permits, and visit their highest-ranking public official, Newtown First Selectman Patricia Llodra.

It had been a long winding path that had turned the seventy-one-year-old grandmother into one of the most prominent public figures in Newtown. Growing up with seven siblings at her family farm in South Hadley, Massachusetts, Patricia first became interested in civic duty when she went traveling during the summers of 1958 and 1959. In Jackson, Michigan, she worked beside her uncle,

Carl M. Saunders, who was editor of the town's local newspaper, the *Jackson Citizen Patriot*.

By then, Saunders had already begun making a name for himself as a journalist. On May 16, 1948, as Cold War tensions were building, he wrote an editorial under the headline, "Suppose All America Prayed for Peace." The article called on all religions to unite in common prayer, saying: "A troubled Christian nation should turn to prayer. Its people should lift their voices as from a single throat in supplication to the Divine Architect of our destinies, remembering always, 'Thy will be done.'"

The editorial spurred a national debate leading to a national day of prayer and was later awarded a Pulitzer Prize, but the takeaway for Patricia was how one editorial from one small town could affect change on a national level.

"I was taken aback by the influence he had. It was just amazing," Patricia later recalled.

She took that experience home to Massachusetts and went on to earn a place at the University of Bridgeport, becoming the first person in her family to go to college. Her education was interrupted when she married Robert M. Llodra in 1963. Within the next few years the couple had three children, Michael, Sharon, and Beth, and began looking for a town with a good school system.

"We visited Sandy Hook Elementary before we decided to buy a house in Newtown and we couldn't have been more impressed," Patricia said. "It was a big part of the reason we moved to Newtown. We wanted our kids to go to the Sandy Hook Elementary School."

The young family moved into an old farmhouse on Riverside

Drive, close to the school, and seventeen years after dropping out of school, Patricia went back to earn her degree. She received praise for her roll-up-the-sleeves no-nonsense management style as she worked through several jobs, including waitress, bartender, teacher, principal, and executive coach, until eventually making the leap into politics.

Patricia was first elected to Newtown's Legislative Council in 2005, and easily won reelection in 2007. In 2009, she ran on the ballot for first selectman, running on a platform of disciplined spending, and defeated Gary Fetzer, who served on the local board of selectmen, by 1,672 votes. Two years later, Patricia campaigned for a second term, espousing the continued need to get Newtown's fiscal house in order. The town overwhelmingly voiced their approval and she defeated William Furrier, a candidate on the Independent ballot, by 3,600 votes.

As Patricia sat at her desk on Friday morning, December 14, she turned on her computer and opened up her schedule to decide how to best manage the challenges of the day ahead. The second week of December had been a busy one full of long meetings and lots of number crunching for Newtown's chief executive and administrative officer. Next year's budget still hadn't been finished and an urgency had set in about completing the task before the upcoming Christmas break.

Then the phone rang. It was Maureen Will, the director of communications.

"The schools are going into lockdown," she said. Maureen hung up, promising to get more information to her as soon as it became available.

This is serious, Patricia thought, waiting by her phone for more information.

She wouldn't be waiting long.

Across the hall, the deputy director of land use, Rob Sibley, was sitting in a meeting opposite Donna Culbert, the public health director. They were discussing the pending approval of a residential sewer when Rob's pager went off. He decided to ignore it and continue with the meeting. Debbie Aurelia, the town clerk, had also stopped by the office, and now the three found themselves talking nonchalantly about the bone-chilling weather that morning.

Like most people who came to Newtown, Rob Sibley and his wife, Barbara, chose the town because of the affordable country living and small-town lifestyle all within a commutable distance to New York City—and, of course, because of the fantastic reputation of Sandy Hook Elementary. In 2004, their first child, Daniel, was born, and three years later Barbara gave birth to twin boys. In Newtown, Rob was able to indulge his lifelong dream—he had always wanted to be a firefighter—and become an EMT at the Sandy Hook Volunteer Fire & Rescue Company in addition to his government job, while Barbara continued working in advertising and began a freelance writing career.

In a short time, the family forged roots in the community. Rob's mother, Jane Sibley, was a minister of visitation at Newtown United

Methodist. His father, Rob Sr., was a retired police officer from nearby New Canaan. Life couldn't have been better for the young family.

"We found Newtown. We couldn't believe our good fortune. We felt like we had stumbled on such a little gem, a real diamond in the rough," Barbara explained.

They also fell in love with the school, Sandy Hook Elementary. "It was just the ideal place."

Rob was still sitting in his office when Donna Culbert, who had left the meeting momentarily, walked back into the room. She had a concerned look on her face. She had heard something on the police scanner in a nearby room about shots being fired at Sandy Hook Elementary School. "Something has happened at Sandy Hook," she told Rob. "Don't you have a child who goes there?"

Rob picked up his pager and looked at the message he had ignored earlier. It was an alert from the fire department. There had been a shooting at the school.

"I have to go," he said and he began walking to his car.

His phone rang. He picked up. It was Barbara. Her voice was shaky. She had been at the school's front entrance, about to drop off the Harry Potter book their third-grade son had left at home, when the sound of gunshots rang out.

"I don't know what you know or what you heard," she said. "I'm hiding behind a Dumpster."

"I know something's going on at the school," Rob told her. "I'm on my way. Just pay attention to what's going on."

CHAPTER 8

FIVE MINUTES, 154 BULLETS

The pair of second-grade students was in the middle of a heated argument outside their classroom on the morning of December 14 when a stern voice froze them in midsentence: "Be nice to each other."

The voice belonged to Principal Dawn Hochsprung, and her words resonated with conviction throughout the halls and into the classrooms where most of the 430 children at Sandy Hook Elementary School had already taken their seats and were ready to begin their day. It was part of the familiar catchphrase that all her students had grown to know so well. She employed it often, reciting it to those she stopped in the hallways, repeating it to the children eating lunch in the cafeteria, and sometimes even mentioning it in passing to parents and colleagues.

Be kind. It's really all that matters.

For many, it would be the last voice they would hear before the intercom was switched on and morning announcements began.

First-grade teacher Kaitlin Roig was sitting at her desk deep in thought over the perfection of the morning. Before school that day, the first thing she'd noticed was the brilliant orange-red sunrise. It was an inspiring sight as it rose up over the water outside her Greenwich, Connecticut, apartment. Feeling the need to capture the moment, she pulled out her phone and snapped a picture before making the fifty-five-mile trek along I-84 east to Newtown.

Over her six years as a teacher at Sandy Hook Elementary, the lively twenty-nine-year-old had earned a reputation as a hard worker who was always willing to take the initiative. When Principal Dawn had been looking for someone to start a running club to promote healthy lifestyles at Sandy Hook earlier in the year, Kaitlin jumped at the opportunity, forming "Marathon Mondays," a running club for the third- and fourth-grade students. The club was a hit. With the positive support of their teacher, the group of children began running one-mile stretches every Monday through the lush green space surrounding Sandy Hook. By June 4 they had already met their goal for the year of 26.2 miles.

Kaitlin waited for the secretary to finish the morning announcements over the intercom. Then at 9:30 A.M. she stood up with her class, faced the American flag above the doorway, and with right hands over their hearts, they recited the Pledge of Allegiance in unison. Kaitlin took attendance and then gathered her fifteen children in a circle on the floor as she did every day.

The "Morning Meeting" was an opportunity for the students to greet each other, share some news of interest to the class, and learn about the day ahead. Kaitlin couldn't imagine a pleasanter way to begin each day than to be surrounded by all her favorite little faces as they shared their own ideas and thoughts.

Teacher Victoria Soto began her day in one of her favorite places, the school library. She was in search of just the right book for her first-grade class when she spotted her colleague Yvonne Cech, a librarian.

"I need to find the perfect book," Victoria said as she explained that she had to read it out loud to her class later that day in front of the parents.

Yvonne walked over to a nearby shelf and returned a short moment later with *What Do You Do with a Tail Like This?* by Steve Jenkins and Robin Page, a children's book that explores amazing things animals can do with their ears, eyes, mouths, noses, feet, and tails.

"The class will love it," Victoria said. "Thanks." She checked the book out before making the short walk from the library to her room.

As the children began to file into her bright and colorful classroom, Victoria greeted them with a cheerful smile. The walls were decorated with paper snowmen cut out of white construction paper, each with the name of the first-grade student prominently displayed so that the little ones could proudly point out their creations when their parents arrived to help make gingerbread houses that afternoon.

After the morning announcements had finished, Victoria looked around the room at all the smiling faces and asked: "Who's excited?"

The class shouted back in a unified roar: "I am!"

• • •

As first-grade teacher Lauren Rousseau waited for class to begin, she texted back and forth with her boyfriend, Tony Lusardi, over their plans that night to see *The Hobbit*.

"Are you ready for the big night?" he texted her at 8:58 A.M.

Her students had long known Rousseau was a huge fan of all things Hobbit-related. The self-confessed "sci-fi dork" had been counting down the days until the release of the new J.R.R. Tolkien movie, a prequel to the *Lord of the Rings* trilogy. After the movie, the couple had plans to go straight to a *Lord of the Rings* themed birthday party for one of her best friends. For the occasion Lauren had already baked "Hobbit" cupcakes with plastic pictures of the different actors embedded in the frosting.

"Of course I'm ready," she had replied. "Woot! Woot! Let's go!"

On the windowsill sat a line of Christmas ornaments left out to dry overnight that the children had made the day before to take home to their parents to decorate their trees. After the morning announcements, the public-address system shut off and Rousseau turned her attention to her students.

In the conference room across the hall, a team of fourth-grade teachers had just sat down to begin their weekly grade-level meeting when in walked Principal Dawn carrying a box of chocolates. The principal caught the four teachers in midconversation, raving about the previous evening's Winter Concert. They were all in absolute awe of the show put on by their students.

"The kids did a great job," Principal Dawn agreed, before spotting teacher Ted Varga's neckwear, a green-and-red Christmas tie, and smiling. "Cute," she jabbed, playfully.

The room broke out in laughter, in part a reaction to her dry sense of humor but more so because it was the kind of easy-breezy morning when laughter didn't need a reason. The entire school was in full-blown holiday mode. In the corner of the small conference room lay gift-wrapped presents collected by the school for children in need. Even the Sandy Hook colors, white and green, blended nicely with the handmade red holiday decorations plastered about the classroom walls.

It was a beautiful morning. The air was crisp, the sky was blue. "The perfect morning," Varga would later recall.

Principal Dawn was on her way to a parent-teacher conference. She walked the short distance to the main conference room where her A team of educators were already seated around a long table: school psychologist Mary Sherlach, lead teacher Natalie Hammond, reading consultant Becky Virgalla, school therapist Diane Day, math/science specialist Kris Feda, as well as a parent.

"Good morning, how are we today?" Dawn asked as she scanned their faces before sitting down at the head. "Looks like everyone is here and ready to go." She dropped her notepad down on the table in front of her and gripped her pen with her right hand. "Let's begin."

Some time before 9:30 A.M. Adam Lanza pulled out of the driveway at 36 Yogananda Street for the last time. Though unconfirmed at the time of this writing, there's reason to suggest that Adam's initial target was the Newtown High School, less than four miles away on Berkshire Road. According to a source familiar with the investigation, Adam Lanza's car was believed to have been identified on the school surveillance footage circling the school parking lot. The official believed Adam spotted two police cars, which were parked in the lot, and decided to move on. The official had not seen the actual footage.

Several minutes later he pulled onto Riverside Road. A right at the Sandy Hook volunteer firehouse on Dickinson Drive and headed toward the elementary school. He drove past the sign that read SANDY HOOK ELEMENTARY. WELCOME VISITORS and made a slight loop around the Sandy Hook parking lot. He pulled to a stop against the vertical yellow lines of the school's fire lane.

It was 9:34 A.M. He was forty feet from the building's main entrance. The parking lot was crowded with cars but no one was coming in or out of the school. No one was milling about. He knew from his years as a student at Sandy Hook Elementary that the morning announcements had just ended and teachers would now be settling their students into the day's routine.

He parked the car with the passenger's side facing the brick wall near the main entrance and left his shotgun leaning against the passenger's side door along with seventy shotgun rounds. If he would later choose to engage law enforcement in either an ambush or subsequent firefight, he would be well positioned.

He climbed out of the driver's seat. Adam left the car doors open and walked at a deliberate pace toward the school's large double doors. The rifle was in his hands. Ten magazines carrying thirty rounds each were in the pockets of his olive green utility vest. Two pistols, the Glock and the Sauer, were in his military-style cargo pants.

Adam was intensely familiar with his surroundings. His memory bordered on photographic and he remembered vividly everything from his days at Sandy Hook Elementary. He'd kept his old report cards and yearbooks. He still had a T-shirt signed by his fifth-grade classmates, even though it had been several years since it last fit him. On occasion, he had even talked to his mom about former teachers and classmates.

Adam hesitated briefly at the entrance. Then stepped back, pointed the rifle at the large plate-glass window to the right of the door, and pulled the trigger eight times. In less than a second, six .223-caliber bullets shattered the glass, creating a hole large enough for him to walk though.

Pop, pop, pop, pop, pop, pop.

The explosion of glass and gunshots echoed throughout the hallways and classrooms of Sandy Hook Elementary, destroying the peace and tranquility of the place forever.

Barbara Halstead, the secretary, was a few feet away in the main office when she heard the violent popping and the sound of crashing glass.

"What's that?" nurse Sally Cox called out from the adjacent infirmary, accessible via a connecting door.

"I don't know," Barbara answered, standing up halfway from her hair.

As the secretary turned her head to investigate, she caught a glimpse of a lanky gaunt figure dressed in black. "Sally!" Barbara called out in a blood-curdling voice as she ducked down underneath her desk.

Broken glass was everywhere. The man was holding a rifle and walking in through the large hole to the right of the door where a glass pane had been. He was coming her way. Sally crouched down low to the floor underneath her computer desk, the alarm in her friend's voice serving as more than enough warning.

Seconds later the gunman walked into the main office and paused, standing quietly only a few feet from where Barbara was hiding. She stayed completely still, barely allowing herself to breathe.

He didn't see her. The gunman turned and walked into the nurse's office. He stood twenty feet from where Sally was hiding underneath her desk. Through the gaps between the furniture and a small hole, she could see a pair of legs from the knees down wearing dark clothing and boots. He was facing in her direction.

The nurse froze in fear. *I'm going to die,* she thought, as she held her breath. *I'm going to die right here and right now.*

Adam did not see her. After a few seconds, he turned and walked back into the hallway. Sally heard the gunman close the door behind him. As he left the main office, Barbara got up from the floor and tried to make her way to the nurse's office. As she began to crawl in that direction, the phone rang. She scurried back across the floor to grab the receiver and in the process inadvertently tripped the microphone to the school public-address system.

"Hello," she said.

"Barb, is everything okay?" a familiar voice on the other end of the line asked.

It was Laura Feinstein, a reading specialist. She had heard the echo of the *pop, pop, pop* all the way from her classroom in the back of the building and knew immediately from the sound of her coworker's voice that something was wrong.

"There's someone in the building shooting," Barbara replied. "Get in lockdown."

Laura ushered her students underneath her computer desk. Barbara hung up the phone and was trying again to crawl to the nurse's office when the phone rang a second time. The secretary picked up the receiver and held it to her ear.

It was a parent, who had no idea there was a gunman in the school. The microphone still on, the entire school was now listening as the secretary began weeping.

"There is a man with a gun. He is shooting inside the school," Barbara pleaded into the receiver. "Oh my God," she continued.

The phone rang a third time. It was Mary Ann Jacob, a library clerk. She had heard the commotion over the school's intercom system and called into the main office to let them know the microphone must have been switched on by accident. Before she could say a word, Barbara told her about the gunman.

"There's a man with a gun," she whispered.

Mary Ann put the phone down. "Lockdown!" she yelled at her eighteen fourth-graders before quickly herding them into a corner of the room. "Get down on the floor and stay quiet," she told them. Mary Ann then ran to the classroom across the hall and told the teacher to lock her door, too.

Still trying to make her way from the main office to the infirmary, Barbara dragged the phone with her as she crawled on her hands and knees across the floor and dialed 911. "Help, we have a shooter," she told the operator. "It's the school. Get help right away."

Seconds later, the secretary and nurse ran together from under their desks into a nearby first-aid supply closet. As they hid, they began to pray.

Principal Dawn Hochsprung instantly knew something was very wrong.

The conference room where the parent-teacher meeting was about to begin was only twenty yards from the school's front entrance, where the noise caused by the explosion of bullets and flying glass had come. Principal Dawn jumped up from her seat and ran out into the hallway, followed closely by her colleagues Mary Sherlach and Natalie Hammond.

Almost immediately after opening the door they were confronted by a nearly unimaginable sight: Adam Lanza, dressed from head to toe in dark clothing, his thin angular face absent of expression and void of all emotion. There were only seconds to react. He was a few feet away and moving toward them, lifting the barrel of a large rifle and pointing it in their direction.

"Shooter. Stay put," Hochsprung screamed to her colleagues still inside the room she had just exited. Her shrill voice was picked up by the live microphone inside the main office and her panicked warning cry was amplified across the entire school via the public-address system.

The principal daringly lunged at the gunman with every inch of her five-foot-two-inch frame, but fell short of reaching the weapon as Adam squeezed the trigger. He shot her at point-blank range. He kept shooting.

Pop, pop, pop, pop, pop, pop, pop, pop, pop, pop, pop.

He struck Principal Dawn several more times. The killer then turned his gun on psychologist Mary Sherlach who had come from the left of the Principal. As Sherlach tried to back away, Adam took aim and unleashed another barrage of bullets in her direction. In total, Adam fired eleven rounds into the hallway, ten with the Bushmaster and one from his pistol.

Seconds after emerging from the conference room, both women now lay dead in the hallway.

Kindergarten aide Deborah Pisani was forty feet down the hallway as the scene unfolded. She was frantically trying to bolt her door, which only locked from the outside, when a ricochet bullet struck her foot. She gasped but managed to restrain her scream as she stumbled back inside the room and took cover.

Lead teacher Natalie Hammond, who had been footsteps behind the slain principal and school psychologist, was also struck in the leg by an errant bullet. She dropped to the ground and lunged back into the conference room where everyone was in a state of panic. The door did not lock. Natalie pulled the handle closed behind her and used her body as a barricade.

"There is a man with a gun. Stay quiet," she told Becky Virgalla, Diane Day, and the parent as the three hid under the table and waited, trying to administer first aid to her wound.

The gunfire filled the corridor with smoke and left the smell of sulfur lingering in the air. The school fell into a quiet hush. The only noise came from Adam Lanza's boots walking with purpose across the floor tiles. Adam had a choice to make: turn left or turn right. To the right, twenty-five children were rehearsing a play in the school cafeteria. To his left were the first-grade classrooms.

Adam Lanza turned left.

In the space of ninety seconds, the reaction of students and faculty inside the building had gone from confusion to alarm and then full-blown terror. The public-address system had amplified the frantic weeping and gasps of secretary Barbara Halstead as she first set eyes on the gunman. Moments later, the entire school had heard the panicked warning screams of Principal Dawn. Then came the unmistakable sound of nine gunshots. An eerie crackling sound now emanated from the speakers as Adam turned the corner and entered the hallway where the first-grade classrooms were located.

The teachers had only one thing on their minds: protect the children.

Kaitlin Roig was still seated in a circle on the floor holding the "Morning Meeting" with her first-grade students when she first heard the violent commotion. *Oh my God, gunshots!* the teacher thought. *This is serious.*

There was no way to protect the class from the sounds. They heard everything: the first shots, the crash of breaking glass, then screams and more gunshots. As the onslaught of terrible noises kept streaming into the class, the children's eyes wandered around the room, toward the window, at each other, until finally settling on their teacher.

"What was that?" one student asked.

"Is it an animal?" questioned another.

"There is an animal loose in the school," yet another child exclaimed.

Kaitlin put her arms high up in the air, drawing all fifteen sets of eyes to her.

"Lockdown! Everyone up, now," she commanded as she rushed to close the classroom door. *Stay calm. The kids need me to stay calm,* she kept telling herself as she tried to keep her motions measured to not further alarm her children.

The teacher closed the door and rounded up her students, quickly shepherding them toward the back end of the room where there was a bathroom. "Let's go! Let's go! Let's go!" she said, her voice beginning to rise as she began physically cramming the children into the small space. As it became apparent that there wouldn't be enough room for all the children to stand, the teacher began lifting some of her smallest students onto the toilet seat and up on the sink so everyone could fit.

"Everyone stay here," she said, before running back out and pushing a wheeled storage shelf in front of the classroom door.

"We are all going to be okay," Kaitlin told her students. "There are bad guys out there now, and now we have to wait for the good guys."

In the classroom directly to the right, Victoria Soto was standing by her desk when the sounds of shots and screams rang out from all around. At first, the strange noises had excited the children, who began frantically chattering back and forth among each other as they tried to make sense of the chaos.

"Is that someone shooting? It sounds like someone shooting a gun," one child said aloud.

"It sounds like the army," another student answered.

The teacher acted to move her fifteen children as far from the danger as possible. "Everyone get away from the door," she shouted, pointing at the far wall. "The wall. Now. Everyone."

The students rarely saw Miss Soto raise her voice, but when she did everyone knew to take it seriously. The children stopped talking and dutifully obeyed, lining up against the wall farthest from the hallway as their teacher hurried to shut the door.

First-grade teacher Lauren Rousseau knew she was in trouble. Her classroom was the third door down the hallway from the main office, on the left. It was directly next to Victoria Soto's and two down from Kaitlin Roig's. Lauren quickly ushered her students toward the back of the room, away from where the sound of screams, popping, and shattering glass were coming.

But locking the door was not an option. Lauren was only a permanent substitute teacher, filling in for the regular first-grade instructor Amanda D'Amato, who was out on maternity leave. Since she was not a full-time staffer, she had not been entrusted with a key. With limited options, Lauren did the only thing left to do. She began leading her students away from the door and toward the corner of the room, near the bathroom.

. . .

Across the school, teachers began initiating the lockdown drills they had diligently practiced only three weeks earlier. Standing down the hallway on the other side of the school with her door open was Pam Midlik, an educational assistant. At first she thought the noise sounded like aluminum unfolding but it continued, stopping and starting. Then the intercom came on in her first-grade classroom and she knew it was something much worse.

An art teacher walked by the door and recognized the sound. "Oh my God, guns! I hear shooting," she said.

A moment later, the two women were joined in the hallway by a father who had arrived to help build gingerbread houses. He was equally terrified. Pam looked at the man and instructed him to go to his child's class and warn the teacher. "Go back to the classroom and tell the teacher it's a lockdown, and close the door and keep the kids safe," she told him before running back into her own room and setting the lockdown drill into motion.

A metal clang echoed down the hallway as Adam, fresh from killing the principal and school psychologist, emptied his magazine, which still contained fifteen live rounds. He loaded a fresh thirty-round clip into his Bushmaster rifle. As he made a left turn and paced down the first-grade corridor, the first classroom Adam reached was where Kaitlin Roig was cowering with her fifteen students.

The children were still crammed inside the bathroom. They

were quiet. The wheeled storage unit was parked in front of the door. A black piece of construction paper was taped over the small window in the door, left over from the recent lockdown drill. She had forgotten to remove it.

Adam walked past.

The second classroom that Adam reached belonged to Victoria Soto's class. The door was shut and the children were standing well away from the door, pressed against the far wall. Miss Soto was standing in front of them, her index finger pressed against her lips.

Again, Adam walked past.

Finally Adam's gaze rested upon the third door on the left-hand side of the corridor. He knew the classroom well. It was where he had sat as a first-grader.

Now it was Lauren Rousseau's class. As he opened the door, the young teacher was still furiously trying to shepherd her fifteen students into the back corner of the room near the bathroom. She turned around to look at the killer and was instantly shot in the face. Then he shot her again.

The students let out terrified screams and clutched each other as the teacher fell to the ground.

He then pointed his Bushmaster and began firing indiscriminately into the group of helpless children, striking special education teacher Rachel Marie D'Avino, killing Catherine Hubbard, Ana Marquez-Greene, James Mattioli, Grace McDonnell, Josephine Gay, Noah Pozner, Jack Pinto, Chase Kowalski, Madeleine Hsu, Jessica Rekos, Daniel Barden, Charlotte Bacon, Benjamin Wheeler, Emilie Parker, and Caroline Previdi.

Amid the chaos and bloodshed, one little girl crouched silently in the corner of the classroom's small bathroom as the killer fired round after round into the children and teachers.

Adam emptied his clip, which still had rounds left, and loaded a fresh one with thirty more rounds. Less than forty seconds after opening the door, Adam turned around and walked out, closing the door behind him.

Inside the school the vacuum of silence that followed the initial flurry of gunfire was now being filled by haunting moans. The sound poured out through the intercom and into every classroom.

A short distance away, separated by only two walls, Kaitlin Roig was convinced she was going to die. The shooting seemed to go on and on until the terrified screams of the children had been dulled to steady groans.

"If anyone believes in the power of prayer, we need to pray, and for those who don't believe in prayer, we need to think happy thoughts," she told her students.

Was the gunman coming for her classroom next? There was no way for the teacher to know from behind the locked door of the dark bathroom where she was huddled with all the children.

"Everyone needs to be absolutely quiet," she continued, her tone measured. "It's going to be okay."

If the gunman was going to shoot his way through her door she knew there wouldn't be much she could do, but she was determined to make sure the final words and sounds the children heard were not groans and gunshots.

"I love you," she kept repeating to her students. "Your parents love you."

. . .

All across Sandy Hook Elementary School, teachers and students were trying to stay calm, trying to comprehend what was unfolding. The second-graders in Carol Wexler's class had just finished their yoga and jumping jacks when the first gunshots rang out. At first the children thought they heard hammers falling or pots and pans clanging, but Carol instantly knew it was something else. Now they were gathered together on the floor, in the dark, amid their puffy winter jackets, waiting.

"Everyone needs to be very quiet," she said in a whisper. "Keep all eyes on me."

She had herded her eighteen students into the corner near their coat hooks before quickly running back to close the classroom door, which also did not lock. Carol shut off the lights. To comfort the children, she began singing holiday songs in a low voice. The children murmured along quietly. "Jingle Bells." "Silent Night." "I Have a Little Dreidel." They did not pause when they heard shots or screams. Some of the children reached into their backpacks for dolls, stuffed animals, worn blankets, anything that gave them comfort.

As they waited, Wexler held one crying girl in her lap, patiently trying to soothe her because the sounds were still coming through the intercom.

The eighteen students in Janet Vollmer's kindergarten class had been hiding in a nook between a pair of bookcases and a wall when the popping noises were replaced by the sick screams of agony.

"Mrs. Vollmer, I'm scared," one student said.

When the kids asked her where the haunting sounds were coming from, at first she tried to blame it on the custodian. "He's probably just on the roof getting a soccer ball," she told them while calmly locking the classroom door, covering the windows, and moving the kids into their hiding place. She then began reading them a story. But as the noises became clearer, there was little the teacher could do to protect them from the harsh reality any longer.

"Some people, they have a stomachache," one little girl said aloud, trying to provide an explanation.

As the children became increasingly restless, the teacher projected calm.

"How come we're here for so long?" the children asked.

"Well, it will be a little longer," she answered. "We're going to be safe, because we're sitting over here and we're all together."

Third-grade teacher Connie Sullivan tried soothing words of comfort while the havoc outside was playing out. "Your mommies and daddies will be here soon," the teacher told her students, who were huddled close together in the corner of the room. "You are loved."

Meanwhile, second-grade teacher Abbey Clements continued to sit with her students in the corner of her classroom, reading aloud.

"Mrs. Clements, you're shaking," one student observed.

A few of the children were crying. Others sat still, looking shocked. Some asked for their moms. Their teacher kept reading.

Moments earlier, when Clements first heard the loud banging

noises, she thought it was folding chairs falling over. She poked her head out into the hallway to get a better look and saw the custodian running full stride down the hallway, along with two students who had been on their way to the office to drop off the class attendance sheet. Both looked rigid with fear.

One of the children, third-grader Bear Nikitchyuk, thought he heard someone kicking a door as he approached the room where the secretary normally sat. As he fled in the opposite direction, he looked back and saw smoke coming from around the corner where the office was located.

Abbey grabbed the two students by their arms and yanked them into her classroom, then ran to get her keys, locked the door, and dialed 911. The custodian continued running from room to room, warning anyone he could find.

"Everyone go to the place where we practice going in emergencies," the teacher told her students as they piled against the far wall near the closets.

As noise from the intercom system kept funneling unfiltered through the room, she kept reading, trying in vain to raise her voice loud enough to muffle what they were hearing.

How do I stop these sounds? These children shouldn't be hearing these sounds, she kept thinking to herself.

Down the hall, music teacher Maryrose Kristopik had just pushed play on the DVD of *The Nutcracker* when they first heard the gunshots, then the screams and cries through the public-address system.

"Everyone hold hands," she told her students, a group of nine- and ten-year-olds, as she walked them single file into a large storage closet in the back of the room where instruments were kept. She handed them all lollipops to help keep them from talking and spoke in a hushed tone. "Everything is going to be okay," she told her students before asking them to hold on to instruments to keep their hands occupied.

Nine-year-old Nicholas Sabillon held on tightly to a gong as he sucked on his lollipop. *This might be the last snack I'm ever going to have,* he thought.

The class continued to hold hands, hug, and wait, trying to block out what they were hearing.

In Teri Alves's third-grade class all the children were crouched in the corner, most of them whimpering for their parents.

"It's going to be okay," she kept repeating in a whisper. "Just stay quiet."

When she first heard the gunshots Alves had moved fast, especially for someone who was eight months' pregnant. In under a minute she had locked the door to her classroom, turned off the lights, and taped a piece of white paper over the window.

"This will all be over soon," the teacher promised. "I need your patience."

Art teacher Leslie Gunn was busy trying to comfort her twenty-three students inside a locked storage room. "Something is wrong and we are going to have to stay here," she told the children as she tried to remain calm.

After hearing the commotion through the school intercom, the children became scared and several had begun sobbing.

"I want to go home," a child pleaded.

"I want my mom," cried another.

Leslie spoke soothingly to convey to the children that everything was going to be okay. "You are all so brave," she told them. "I love you."

A few minutes earlier she had been preparing to teach her class how to work with clay and make sculptures. As they began their art project, the public-address system had switched on.

Someone must be working on the roof, Leslie thought, but as the noise grew louder and more persistent she knew that something was horribly wrong. Her hand began shaking as she dialed 911, but after getting a busy signal, she called her husband.

"I don't know what is going to happen to us," she told him.

Still inside the locked first-aid closet off the main office, secretary Barbara Halstead and nurse Sally Cox prayed out loud in hushed tones as they heard the methodical sound of gunfire stop and start.

"Please stop. Please stop."

"Maybe he's not actually hurting anyone," they tried to tell themselves. "Maybe he's just spraying bullets around."

• • •

In the rear of the school building, Laura Feinstein had begun playing games with her students underneath her computer desk. The teacher had hoped the activity would distract them but the sounds from the intercom were too clear and too loud to ignore. She had tried calling 911, but her cell phone didn't have reception so she texted her husband and asked him to call for her as they continued to wait for help.

Shari Burton, a teacher's assistant, was sitting on the floor with her sixteen students in the second-grade classroom on the far side of the building, also trying to get through to 911. When they first heard the shots, the teacher tried desperately to lock the door, but it wouldn't lock. She saw the custodian, Rick Thorne, who shooed them inside the room before running back out into the hall and returning with his master key to lock the door. After securing them in the classroom, Thorne continued running up and down the hallways, warning staff while using the key to ensure the other doors in the hall were locked.

"When is someone coming? When is someone coming?" Burton kept repeating into her cell phone.

"What are you hearing?" the operator asked.

"I'm hearing *pop, pop, pop, pop, pop, pop.* And it isn't stopping."

"Do you think it's gunshots?"

"I think it's gunshots."

"I'm going to put you on hold for a minute, ma'am. There're lots of calls coming in. As long as you're safe—how many people are in the room?"

"Sixteen children and two adults, and we are safe now."

A moment later a text came through to Shari Burton's phone. Finally, she thought. It must be one of the three members of her family who were members of the Sandy Hook Volunteer Fire & Rescue Company, about two hundred yards up the road from the school. She assumed one of them had heard and must be wondering if she was okay. Her husband, Michael Burton, was the department's second assistant chief. Her son, Michael Burton Jr., was a junior member of the department, and her daughter, Kelly Burton, volunteered as a firefighter and was an alumna of Sandy Hook Elementary.

It was twenty-year-old Kelly, who was home from college, but she hadn't heard about the shooting. Instead she wanted to know why her mom hadn't left the car for her to drive.

"Why didn't you wake me up to bring you to school?" her daughter texted.

"There's a shooter in the school. On lockdown," Shari wrote back.

Kelly stared at the message from her mother with confusion. *There is no way*, she thought. *This has to be some kind of joke.*

Then another text came through from her mom: "There were shots fired. A lot of shots."

Chris Manfredonia, an athletic director at the local high school, was walking toward Sandy Hook's main entrance to help make gingerbread houses with his daughter when he saw the front door's glass blown away and smelled the sulfur. He knew right away it was gunfire. Not knowing what the scene was inside the school, he crouched down low and began sprinting to the side of the school where he knew his daughter's second-grade classroom was located.

Thirty yards away, Officers William Chapman and Scott Smith pulled up in front of the school at 9:38 A.M., emerging from the car with weapons drawn.

Adam Lanza walked out of Lauren's classroom and backtracked toward Victoria Soto's classroom. He let his partially used clip drop to the floor, exchanging it for a fresh one. The first-graders pressed against the far wall were in the throes of complete panic. The sounds of the killings had been coming at them from all directions, echoing through the intercom above and from behind the wall only feet from where they were standing. They could hear the children screaming, the pleas for life, and the popping sound of the Bushmaster rifle before it gave way to the sustained groans of the dying.

The door opened slowly and for a brief moment the man dressed in black with the pale, gaunt face and the long rifle stood still in the doorway, surveying the class. As he looked at the students, his face was expressionless. Standing at the back of the room near the window was their teacher, Victoria Soto. Before she had time to utter a single word, Adam had turned to his left, pointed his rifle at the young teacher and pulled the trigger.

Her body fell to the ground, landing near her desk.

The children broke ranks from their positions next to the wall where they were instructed to stand and began running around the room crying and screaming. Some of the children had gathered in the far right corner of the room near the chalkboard and began holding hands, quietly whimpering to each other.

With the cries and pleas for mercy muffled by his earplugs, Adam aimed his rifle at random children as they scurried about the room. Then the gunman set his sights on Allison Wyatt, Avielle Richman, Olivia Engel, and special education teacher Anne Marie Murphy. Murphy had put her arms around six-year-old Dylan Hockley in an attempt to shield him from the bullets. Lanza fired at them, shooting and killing them both. They all slumped to the floor in pools of blood.

Then the shooting stopped. Adam's rifle had jammed. First-grader Jesse Lewis, who was standing behind the children holding hands, stared directly at the shooter and shouted: "Run!" Four did run, squeezing past the killer standing in the doorway. Two other students ran into the bathroom.

As the gunman turned his head, six-year-old Aiden Licada, seven-year-old Bryce Maksel, and two of their friends also ran straight past Adam and out the door.

Adam paused to reload. Then the gunman turned to Jesse and fired a single shot into the brave child's head, killing him instantly.

Pop, pop, pop, pop, pop, pop.

Outside the school, Officers Chapman and Smith took cover behind their police cruiser. They had heard a report that someone was shooting outside the school. The shots were loud. They desperately looked around, trying to find out where the gunfire was coming from.

• • •

Across the hall from the first-grade classrooms, the fourth-grade teachers had finally stopped marveling at the previous night's successful Winter Concert and were getting down to the agenda for their team meeting. The harsh cacophony of gunshots and screaming had just flooded the room when suddenly the door burst open.

It was Rick Thorne, the custodian. "You need to hide," he told them, his voice full of adrenaline. "There is a man with a gun in the school."

The teachers weren't used to seeing Thorne in the school at that time of day. It was a shift Thorne rarely worked but had agreed to cover for his supervisor, Kevin Antonelli, who was out on vacation. The custodian had been on the far side of the building when he first heard the gunfire and had immediately taken off in a full sprint toward the mayhem. As he turned a corner he had seen the two bodies of his friends, the principal and school psychologist, lying on the floor in pools of blood. He had already dialed 911 and was now going from room to room to warn the school.

Just as quickly as he had entered the meeting room, he was gone. Thorne had closed the door and continued running through the hallways, shouting that there was a "man with a gun," and turning all the door handles to make sure they were secured.

The fourth-grade teachers were divided over what to do next. Ted Varga looked around the room. There was no lock. There was no place to hide. *My God,* he thought. *We are only four doors down from the office where the intercom is. We are sitting ducks waiting to be killed.*

Varga believed they needed to make a run for it. "We need to get out! We need to leave," he pleaded. "We can't wait in here. There is no place to hide."

But leaving the security of the room would be foolhardy, his coworkers argued. Kate Anderheggen, Katherine Gramolini, and Carrie Usher wanted to wait in the room for help. To them, it made no sense to run toward the sounds of violence when they weren't in immediate danger.

"Ted, don't do it. Don't go," they begged. "Let's hide here."

In the room next door, there was nothing Kaitlin Roig could do to shield her children from the heart-wrenching sounds. Several of the students, all only six or seven years old, had begun weeping.

"I just want Christmas . . . I don't want to die, I just want to have Christmas," one of the students begged.

"I want to go home," another child pleaded, tears streaming from her eyes.

The teacher cupped the child's small face in her hands and pulled her closer. "I love you," Kaitlin said, unable to conceal the emotion in her voice. "I need you to know that I love you all very much and it's going to be okay."

Their little bodies all crammed in the tiny dark bathroom, her students were beginning to grow restless. It had been only three minutes since the first gunshots had shattered the front entrance glass and she had ushered everyone into the bathroom, but to the students it felt as if they had been crushed together for an eternity.

After this latest round of pops, the only noise anyone could hear was agonized moaning. The children began to whisper quietly to their teacher. Now that it was quiet, maybe they should open the door and take a look?

"Can we go see if anyone is out there?" a student said in a hushed voice.

Another volunteered to guide the class to safety. "I know karate, so it's okay, I'll lead the way out," the brave little student offered. The teacher smiled at the moment of levity.

"Thank you for that," Roig said. "But no one is opening this door."

Silence.

The shooting had finally stopped. The earplugs muffled the sound of the sirens in the distance, but the unmistakable flashing lights from the squad car were visible from the window. With two educators and five innocent children killed by his bullets lying lifeless on the classroom floor, Adam dropped his Bushmaster near the middle of the room and sat down on the floor. Still in the pockets of his vest, Adam had three magazines for the Bushmaster, each containing thirty rounds.

Seconds after 9:40 A.M., less than five minutes after first entering the building, Adam Lanza sat himself up in a corner. With his right hand, he placed the Glock handgun up to his head and pulled the trigger.

After the last shot, an eerie silence overtook the school.

At 9:41 A.M., Officers William Chapman and Scott Smith turned their radios down and entered the school through the front entrance. In the rear of the building, in the library, Mary Ann Jacob had begun coloring with her fourth-graders. The group of eighteen students believed the door was locked until they saw one of the doors open and the barrel of a gun emerge. It was a police officer.

After seeing the look of terror on the police officer's face, Mary Ann realized the danger was far from over. Her students crawled across the floor to a storage room where she passed out paper and crayons and asked them to continue coloring.

Ted Varga had heard enough. He couldn't wait in the room another minute. He first tried to knock out the air conditioner that had been installed in the window. The wood holding the unit in place gave way but the hole wasn't large enough for all of them to fit through. He opened the door of the conference room and peered out. The smell of gunpowder was in the air. He could taste it. He looked both ways and didn't see anyone.

"Follow me! Let's go! Let's go, let's go!" he told his coworkers and ran toward the emergency exit near the front side of the building.

No one followed. Two other teachers were finally able to get through the window, while a third lay hidden under a pile of wrapped gifts, donated for needy children from the school's charity program. She heard someone jiggling the door handle and the sound of heavy breathing.

It's the gunman, she thought. *I'm going to die.*

Seventeen minutes after the first gunshots, a voice was heard through the school intercom: "It's okay. It's safe now."

————◄◦►————

CHAPTER 9

FIRST RESPONDERS

Two miles away, inside the Newtown police station, Officer William Chapman had been sitting at his desk doing paperwork. It had been the kind of lazy Friday morning he had come to expect from this quiet town of 27,000. A handful of traffic tickets and maybe a few runs on domestic disputes could be expected. A mild stir had come earlier in the month after resident Laurie Borst believed she'd spotted a fisher cat on her property. The large predatory member of the weasel family had circled her yard holding a squirrel in its mouth before it scurried away. The story was front-page news on the local weekly newspaper the *Newtown Bee*.

In Newtown, big news did not come often. It had been nearly three decades since the town had experienced its last murder. The case of Mary Elizabeth Heath began in April 1984, when she was first reported missing from her Newtown home by her husband,

John Heath. Twenty-six years after the missing-person report, a man and his son were renovating an apartment in a barn on Poverty Hollow Road once owned by John Heath. In a cistern under the floor they found Mary Elizabeth Heath's bones. More of her remains were found stuffed in bedding.

The investigation revealed that Mary Elizabeth had died from blunt-force trauma to the head and that she had two broken arms, wounds that probably came as she put her arms up to defend herself. Police charged John Heath with murder. He pleaded not guilty and awaits trial. The break in the cold case was the biggest event to have happened in the town that anyone could remember.

The first call came in at 9:35:52 A.M. from secretary Barbara Halstead. The dispatcher quickly relayed it to the police officers. *"Sandy Hook School. The caller is indicating she thinks there's someone shooting in the building."*

Without hesitation, Officer Chapman jumped up and ran to his cruiser with his partner, Officer Scott Smith. Sirens blaring, they hit seventy miles per hour as they drove the three-mile residential stretch from the station to the school, all the while listening intently to their radio as more calls were being relayed through dispatch.

"Someone is shooting in the building."

At 9:36 A.M. another call came in. Again, the dispatcher patched it through to the squad car. *"The individual I have on the phone is continuing to hear what he believes to be gunshots."*

The officers began mentally preparing themselves to storm the school, having been trained to react to active-shooter situations by moving toward the sound of gunfire to neutralize the gunman as quickly as possible.

The car came to a screeching halt in front of the main entrance at 9:38 A.M. The two officers were immediately met with the blasting echoes of gunfire.

It was rifle fire and it was very close. It sounded like it was coming from outside. They jumped out of their seats and took cover behind the squad car. They looked all around for the shooter.

The gunfire stopped.

Then six more shots: *pop, pop, pop, pop, pop, pop.*

9:38:10 A.M.: *"The shooting appears to have stopped. The school is in lockdown."*

A few seconds of silence. Then three more shots were fired. *Pop, pop . . . pop.*

Officers Chapman and Smith continued looking around for someone to shoot back at but were still unable to locate the gunman outside.

9:38:50 A.M.: *"We'll stage up the SWAT and go from there."*

Outside the school, ten more law enforcement officers had just arrived, and began taking positions at various entrances. The tactical officers were putting on their vests and grabbing weapons out of their vehicles.

9:39:05 A.M.: *"Reports that teachers saw two shadows running, past the building, past the gym."*

Parent Chris Manfredonia was still in a state of confusion. He was hunched over and walking quickly along the exterior of the school, urgently trying to make his way to the window of his six-year-old daughter's classroom. He kept hearing the gunshots. He was looking through windows, and ducking down, but he couldn't locate her.

Two police officers spotted Manfredonia and, with guns drawn, ordered him to freeze. Manfredonia wasn't taking any chances. He had heard the gunshots and didn't know if the men in uniform were law enforcement or murderers. He paused momentarily then took off running, first taking a right past the storage shed and then bolting up into the wooded forest with the officers in pursuit close behind.

9:39:20 A.M.: *"Yeah, we got 'em. They're coming at me."*

"Hands up! Hands up!" the police ordered. "Get down!"

"I'm a parent," Manfredonia answered. "I'm a parent!"

He slowly raised his hands up in the air and got down on his knees.

Leonard Penna, a school resource officer who had raced to the scene from his office at the Newtown Middle School, took his position with Sergeant Aaron Bahamonde and Lieutenant Christopher Vanghele near a side door that leads to the boiler room. Officer Michael McGowan and two other officers took their positions at a locked door in the rear of the building. One of them knocked out the glass with his rifle butt so the rest of the officers could get in; as soon as they heard that the second shooter had been found, they entered the school. Officer McGowan was familiar with the lay of the land. He had attended the school as a child.

Chief Michael Kehoe and another officer took their positions at a side entrance. The radios attached to their hips kept feeding them information in an effort to get a handle on the situation they were confronting.

The Newtown Town Hall had gone into lockdown.

Minutes after First Selectman Patricia Llodra had received the phone call from her communications director notifying her of a shooting at Sandy Hook, she left her office and drove straight to the local police department. She walked into the back area where two dispatchers were struggling to keep up with the heavy volume of calls.

Llodra began fielding calls also. Most of them were from anxious parents wanting to know where their children were. She was handed a hastily made script to read from: "We don't yet know the nature of the lockdown. Parents should stay put and wait for more information."

At 9:41 A.M., with the perceived threat of the second gunman neutralized, the officers entered the school. Officers Chapman and Scott turned their radios down low as they slowly made their way to the front entrance, where the glass had been shot out. They entered the front lobby and were immediately confronted with the sight of the first dead, Principal Dawn Hochsprung and school psychologist Mary Sherlach.

After seeing their bodies they spotted Rick Thorne, the custodian, running down the hallway.

"Stop. Put your hands up," they screamed at Thorne with guns drawn.

Thorne stopped fast in his tracks. "Don't shoot. Don't shoot," he answered, his arms raised high.

"Put your hands up! Hands up!" they again commanded.

"I am the custodian. I work here. I'm the custodian," he pleaded.

They ordered Thorne to wait and, with their guns drawn, carefully went from room to room, urgently hunting down the killer or killers before he or they could do more harm.

As Officers Chapman and Smith approached the second classroom in the hallway on their left, they spotted a rifle on the floor. Inside, they found the gunman, Adam Lanza, dead by his own hand, along with the bodies of children Jesse Lewis, Allison Wyatt, Avielle Richman, Olivia Engel, and their teacher, Victoria Soto. They also found the body of teacher Anne Marie Murphy, her arms around her student, six-year-old Dylan Hockley.

Then came the grueling task of searching for signs of life among the children. Officer Chapman found a faint pulse on a little girl, Olivia Engel, who was still faintly breathing. The tall, muscular Chapman cradled the child in his arms and ran with her outside.

"We need a bus!" he screamed.

"You're safe now; your parents love you," he kept repeating to Olivia again and again, trying to comfort her. "The police are here to protect you."

As he walked farther he again shouted for an ambulance. "Get the bus!" Chapman screamed, still trying to comfort the young girl, who lay limp in his arms. Officer Chapman walked a few feet toward the bus before his strength gave out. He collapsed to the ground.

9:40 A.M.: *"You'll need two ambulances."*

The SWAT team had now entered the school and begun searching room by room for the shooter as frantic calls continued coming into dispatch from teachers in the school who believed there could be more shooters on the loose.

9:40:30 A.M.: *"Shooter's apparently still shooting in office area. Dickinson Drive."*

Not long after volunteer firefighter and EMT Kelly Burton read the chilling text message from her mom saying, "There's a shooter in the school," she received a call dispatching her to the scene. Her house was several miles away and her mother, Shari, was still trapped inside the school.

"We just got dispatched," Kelly texted her mom.

The thought of her daughter being anywhere near Sandy Hook horrified Shari. She pleaded with her child not to come. "I don't want you to come. Stay home. Too many shots, I don't want you to come," pleaded her mother.

"I'm coming. It doesn't matter what you say, I'm going to find a way there," Kelly fired back.

Kelly hitched a ride to the nearby firehouse and geared up. At the firehouse she spotted her father, Michael Burton, the department's second assistant chief.

"Where do you want me to go?" she asked him.

"Are you okay?" he asked back.

"I'm fine. What do you want me to do?"

"Go out back and see what help they need with the triage," he answered.

Kelly walked back to the school where the triage had already been set up. She knew four patients had been transported to the hospital and that dozens remained inside. She waited outside, along with an army of first responders from neighboring areas ready to treat all the injured children.

Why aren't they coming out? she thought to herself. *Where are the children?*

9:40:55 A.M.: *"Troop Eight personnel, take exit 10, left on 34, turn on Riverside Drive. Make sure you have your vests on."*

Officer Penna was the first cop to enter the second room. At first he couldn't process the carnage that appeared in front of him. Huddled together in the corner of the room were teachers Lauren Rousseau and Rachel Marie D'Avino, along with students Catherine Hubbard, Ana Marquez-Greene, James Mattioli, Grace McDonnell, Josephine Gay, Noah Pozner, Jack Pinto, Chase Kowalski, Madeleine Hsu, Jessica Rekos, Daniel Barden, Charlotte Bacon, Benjamin Wheeler, Emilie Parker, and Caroline Previdi.

They were all found wrapped together, clutching each other for comfort during their final moments. Each had suffered multiple gunshot wounds. The scene was too horrific to be from this earth, he thought.

Officer Penna walked over and began checking for life amid the bodies and found a single girl standing alone, covered from head to toe in blood. She appeared to be in shock but had not been injured.

"Stay where you are," the officer told the child, not knowing of possible threats still in the school. "I'll be right back."

He ran into the next classroom and saw the dead gunman, with Officers Chapman and Smith standing nearby. Officer Penna returned to the second classroom, his rifle slung around his chest, grabbed the uninjured girl by the arm and ran with her out to a triage area set up in the parking lot.

Sgt. William Cario and Trooper Patrick Dragon had rerouted to Sandy Hook from a narcotics task force meeting nearby after hearing the initial reports of a shooting on their police radio. After coming upon the Hellish scene inside of Rousseau's room, the officers each grabbed an injured child and ran outside where a cruiser was waiting to rush the children to Danbury Hospital. Both would later die there.

Officers entered the conference room where the parent-teacher meeting had been about to take place and found Natalie Hammond. They made sure her coworkers were applying proper first aid to the bullet wound in her leg and moved on in their search for more survivors and another possible gunman.

9:46:20 A.M.: *"We've got an injured person in room 9 with numerous gunshot wounds."*

Lieutenant Christopher Vanghele, the incident commander on the scene until Connecticut State Police assumed control, began relaying the unimaginable scope of the tragedy to his colleagues.

9:49:05 A.M.: *"Negative on description. Shots were fired about three minutes ago."*

9:53:25 A.M.: *"Newtown's reporting one suspect down. The building has now been cleared."*

Adam Lanza's body was slumped down against the floor. A large pool of blood had settled near what remained of his face.

The earplugs were still in his ears. Near his right hand rested the 10-millimeter Glock handgun that he had used to fire the final bullet into his own head.

Officers carefully checked Adam Lanza's body for explosives. They found the cache of unspent clips for the Bushmaster, each capable of firing thirty rounds, along with the 9-millimeter SIG Sauer P226 handgun, fully loaded.

In his pockets they found a driver's license—the name read "Ryan Lanza."

Within minutes, officers from the state police, the FBI, the ATF, the U.S. Marshals Service, and other agencies arrived on the scene. Of the forty-five police officers in the Newtown Police Department, fourteen went into Sandy Hook Elementary School. In addition to the triage area that responders had already set up outside the school doors others set up an area at a nearby fire station where parents were reunited with their children.

Dad Chris Manfredonia was handcuffed and walked to the front of the school where a group of parents had now gathered, waiting for their children. The worried moms and dads suspiciously eyed the handcuffed man, who was dressed in camouflage pants and wearing a dark jacket.

"I didn't do it," he told them as the police put him in the back of a squad car.

Newtown First Selectman Pat Llodra arrived at the school. She found Newtown Chief of Police Michael Kehoe, who informed her of the scene inside the two classrooms. A feeling of horror and shock ran through her. She took a brief moment to internalize the pain, then, knowing that the eyes of the community would look to her for strength, she searched deep for a place to wall off the rush of emotions.

This can't be real. In a school that did everything right, she thought. She took a deep breath, and then began to try to manage the chaos.

Llodra's town hall coworker, Rob Sibley, a first responder and EMS volunteer at Sandy Hook Elementary, had also arrived at the school. He was gearing up by the truck to enter the school and look for victims to treat. He saw his wife, Barbara, and they embraced.

Barbara had driven over to the school to drop off their son Daniel's copy of *Harry Potter and the Chamber of Secrets* that he'd left behind and needed for Library Day. As she pulled down the long driveway on Dickinson shortly after 9:35 A.M., she noticed a group of children running along the side of the road. They weren't wearing jackets and were screaming.

That's strange. I wonder where their teacher is? she thought. Sibley assumed the children were part of the local running club. *That's funny. I thought the running club was on Wednesday not Friday.*

As she continued looking, one of the young boys had pulled away from the group and was screaming, "Don't go to the school! Don't go in!"

Sibley parked her car and opened the car door, then heard three loud bangs, followed by silence. Still baffled, she thought, *Someone must be working on the roof.*

Outside the school Sibley noticed an eerie silence. *I can't be-*

lieve how quiet it is, she thought as she walked from her car to the school's main entrance. *Where are all the kids?*

As she approached the front door where visitors had to be buzzed in, she noticed a black car parked in the fire lane to her right. Its doors were all open and black sweatshirts were strewn around it. *That's really odd,* she thought. *You usually don't see that at a school.*

As she got closer to the door, she spotted another mother, Karyn Holden. She was staring in confusion at the front entrance.

"Is something going on here?" Barbara asked.

"I don't know, but look," Karyn answered, pointing to the shattered glass and missing window to the right of the front door.

"Well, this is very strange," replied Barbara. The entire front window panel next to the door was missing. Tiny shards of glass were sprinkled everywhere. She poked her head in a little farther, looking for a rock or something that could have shattered a hole that large but couldn't find one.

"Do you think we should go in?" Karyn asked.

Barbara began to open her mouth, but before she could get the first syllable out, an eruption of sound came from inside the building. Gunshots. It was loud. And it sounded as if it was very close.

Pop. Pop. Pop. Pop. Pop. Pop. Pop.

The two women ducked down and ran to take cover behind the nearby Dumpsters about twenty feet away. There was a pause. Then the popping sound continued. One shot after another in a methodical pattern.

That's gunfire. My child, thought Sibley. *Do I run into the path of the gunfire and try to save my son? Or do I stay alive for my two children at home?*

Another pause, followed by more gunshots.

I wouldn't be able to save anyone inside. I need to live for my children, she answered herself.

She needed to call her husband. She searched for her phone but realized she had left it in her car. Karyn had her phone and had begun making calls. She handed it to Barbara who, not being able to remember her husband's phone number, dialed her mother.

"Mom, I don't want to alarm you, but I'm at the school and I think there has been a shooting. I have to go, but I'm hiding behind a Dumpster and I'm going to be all right."

Her confused mother, at a loss for words, answered, "Okay."

She then called her boss. "Hi, Chris, it's Barb. How are you?"

Her superior returned the greeting.

"I'm okay but someone is shooting inside the school and I'm hiding behind a Dumpster and I'm going to be late to the meeting."

Finally, she remembered her husband Rob's number and called him.

He already knew and was on his way. She looked at Karyn, a stranger just a few minutes earlier who also had a child inside the school. They hugged each other tightly, each saying, "I love you."

After being led to safety, Barbara spotted her husband from behind, putting on his gear. After they embraced, Rob finished getting ready and walked into the building. Word had already spread of the carnage that awaited him inside. He made a quick call to his father, Robert Sibley, a retired police officer.

"I don't know if I can do this," he told his father.

"Rob, you have to. You're a trained professional. You're an EMT. You have to and you can. Trust me."

Rob put his phone away and walked through the front entrance of Sandy Hook Elementary. In the hallway he saw Principal Dawn Hochsprung and Mary Sherlach. A week earlier he had been in a meeting with both of them to discuss his son Daniel. As he approached the classrooms, an officer guarding the room stopped him.

"Spare yourself," the trooper told him.

Rob took the officer's advice.

One veteran law enforcement official had walked into the classroom unprepared for the scene. The children were too much. He recognized one of them. Her family attended the same church. He had seen her just five days earlier. He took his hat off, turned away, and bent over, trying hard not to be sick and contaminate the crime scene.

"I can't. My God," he said, bent down to the ground with his hands on his knees, trying to catch his breath. "Oh my God. Oh my God. Children."

A colleague came over and helped him get back to his feet and escorted him out of the building.

Three officers, in full uniform, had collapsed on the ground outside of the classroom of Lauren Rousseau. They couldn't catch their breath. They couldn't move, paralyzed by the graphic scene inside. Two other state troopers who had looked inside the classrooms walked outside the school and stood for a minute before embracing each other. Tears began to roll down their cheeks and their chests began rising and falling heavily as they openly sobbed.

Nearby dispatchers continued warning of more gunmen and flooded the area with local ambulances.

9:55:25 A.M.: *"Be advised, we have multiple weapons. One rifle and a shotgun."*

9:57:25 A.M.: *"Any plainclothes responding, make sure you have your raid gear on, your raid gear on."*

10:00:15 A.M.: *"Ask the custodian, get a team up on the roof and clear the roof."*

10:00:40 A.M.: *"We need [inaudible] up here right away. Call Danbury if you have to."*

The Newtown Police Department's emergency operations center was quickly transformed from an emergency response center into an investigative operations center. Investigators from a number of agencies set up shop there, combing social media Websites for clues. A judge was on hand to sign off on search warrants. Privately, the police were telling each other to be prepared for up to sixty casualties.

10:03 A.M.: *"What is the number of ambulances you will require?" "They don't know, they're not giving us a number."*

10:04:40 A.M.: *"You might want to see if surrounding towns can send EMS personnel. We're running out pretty quick."*

Eight minutes later, at 10:12 A.M., they had begun setting up another triage area near the firehouse.

10:28 A.M.: *"Roger, closet in the kitchen, you have some victims. Let us know, we'll call the number so you know they're coming."*

"Call for everything."

"Do you know if anyone brought a mass casualty kit?"

An officer grabbed a roll of yellow tape and used it to quarantine the black Honda Civic that was parked in the fire lane. A second officer stood guard by the car as another carefully removed the loaded Izhmash Saiga-12 combat shotgun from the passenger seat compartment and placed it in the trunk of the car. After investigators entered the Honda's license plate number into the Department of Motor Vehicles database, it took under thirty seconds before a name and address came back. The plate 872 YEO was registered to Nancy Lanza of 36 Yogananda Street.

It was only five miles away. State police were already en route.

Meanwhile, the officers continued their search of the school, using the master key given to them by custodian Rick Thorne to search room to room. With state troopers coming in, police began to evacuate the children who were still behind locked doors. One of the officers, full of adrenaline, accidentally snapped the key in one of the clasroom doors. Many of the teachers, seeking to protect their students and following their own training, refused to open up.

Art teacher Leslie Gunn and her twenty-three students had been waiting inside a storage cabinet for fifteen minutes when they heard someone banging loudly on the door.

"Police. It's okay to open up," a voice through the door announced.

Before opening the door the teacher instructed her students to "hold each other's hands and not let go."

As officers continued their room-to-room search they found the bathroom door locked in Kaitlin Roig's classroom.

"Police," an officer said through the door. "It's okay to come out now. You can open the door."

Kaitlin wanted proof before she unlocked her door. "I don't believe you," she yelled back. She was concerned that it could be a trick by the gunmen to lure them out. "You are going to have to show me some identification before I open this door. Slide your badges under the door," she told them.

After an officer slid his badge to her, Kaitlin still was not sold. "If you really are a police officer, you would have a way in here, you would have a key."

A few minutes later the police retrieved the key and opened the door before escorting the class to safety. As the children emerged, the officers tried to reassure them in their best calm, fatherly voices.

"Everything is fine now," they said, even as they stayed alert for a possible second gunman. "Everybody hold hands, close your eyes," they told the children as they led them past the carnage.

Some officers formed a human curtain around the bodies of Ms. Hochsprung and Ms. Sherlach, to shield the children from the sight as they walked past. Others blocked the doorways of the two classrooms. The children came out in single-file lines, eyes closed, hands clutching each other by the shoulders. Police at all sides, teachers in front and back.

Outside, armored cars and ambulances and countless police officers swarmed with dogs and roared overhead in helicopters. As new officers continued to arrive, they were warned by the officers standing guard outside the school about the scene inside.

"If you have children, you especially don't want to go in there," they advised.

Detective Joe Joudy looked at Officer Chapman, covered in blood, walking back inside the school. "They've got to get you guys out of here," he told Chapman.

Ambulances from within a twenty-mile radius continued racing toward the scene, making a long line up Dickinson Drive. As time passed, EMS workers, many who had children, or had known children, inside the school, had flooded the scene and were anxiously holding their breath, hoping to provide medical assistance to the injured survivors.

Then came the call that no one wanted to hear.

The Newtown EMS captain ordered all ambulances and first responders to stand down. This was followed by a horrifying revelation. The directive meant that police were not expecting to find many survivors among the victims. There was no one left to help, no one left alive.

"Hold all other ambulances."

CHAPTER 10

———◁◦▷———

SOMETHING IS WRONG
AT SANDY HOOK

Parent Tricia Gogliettino was driving to Sandy Hook Elementary School Friday morning to deliver a gingerbread house she and her first-grade daughter had made together. The previous night she had been at Newtown High School with her brother John Frey to watch her daughters perform in the Winter Concert.

"At the Sandy Hook Elementary School holiday concert cheering nieces, Joan and Bridget," he had tweeted from the concert hall.

When Gogliettino got less than a mile from the school, she spotted five young children running in a straight line up Riverside Road. Some of their bare arms were exposed in the frigid morning air. She stopped the car, rolled down her window, and asked the children where they were going.

"Someone is trying to kill us. We were told to run," the children answered.

"Who is trying to kill you?" Tricia asked as she directed the

132

children into her car and called the school. The phone rang several times but no one answered. She called the Newtown police, who told her to bring the children to the police station right away.

Susan Ludwig was also heading to the school to make gingerbread houses with her daughter, a first-grader, when she saw Gogliettino standing in the middle of the road with the five children and pulled over to see if everything was okay.

"Something is really wrong. These boys say someone is trying to kill them," Gogliettino told Ludwig.

"Someone is trying to kill them?" she replied. "My daughters are inside the school."

Shortly before 9:40 A.M., parents districtwide received a voice mail notification that Newtown schools had been put in lockdown, due to a shooting "as yet unconfirmed."

Gene Rosen didn't want to believe what he was hearing. *It can't be true. Not in Sandy Hook,* he kept thinking to himself. But there they were, six young children telling a tale too horrible to have ever been made up.

He had just finished feeding his cats and had walked out the back door on his way to the diner when he first spotted four boys and two girls sitting in a neat semicircle on his front yard, a school bus driver hovering over them. The children were crying and hyperventilating and shivering in the cold without their jackets as the bus driver frantically tried to comfort them. But his nervous tone was only making them more upset.

"It's no problem. I'll take care of them," Rosen told the bus driver. He looked down at the children and smiled warmly. "Come up to my house and we can figure this out while we wait for your parents," he told them, stretching his arms out.

The frightened students didn't say a word as Rosen walked them up the gravel path into the small home that he shared with his wife, Marilyn. Rosen, a retired psychologist; he knew something was very wrong as they walked up the hill in silence, but he didn't ask any questions, not wanting to press the shaken children. His sole focus was to make sure the children felt comfortable until he could get them into the arms of their parents.

He led them inside and settled them down on the rug in front of the couch in his small living room, brought them glasses of juice, then went upstairs and came down with some toys that belonged to his grandchildren before calling the children's parents, using cell phone numbers obtained from the school bus company.

After he had finished making the phone calls, he again directed his attention to the children. They were quiet. Finally, a little boy broke the silence and the room became flooded with pent-up emotion.

"We can't go back to the school. We can't go back to the school. We can't go back to the school," the young boy kept repeating, tears streaming down his face. "We don't have a teacher. Our teacher is dead. Ms. Soto; we don't have a teacher."

After the first child spoke, another boy began to open up about the unspeakable horror he had witnessed with his classmates.

"He had a little gun and a big gun," another boy added.

Then one of the girls began speaking.

"Mrs. Soto. Mrs. Soto. Mrs. Soto is dead. There is blood," she added. "She had blood in her mouth and blood coming out of her mouth and she fell."

All the while Rosen sat silently, listening, trying to remain calm as some of the other children continued describing what sounded more like a sick nightmare than a morning at Sandy Hook Elementary. As they spoke, one little girl sat silently spelling her name out on a stuffed frog that had the alphabet on its belly. Another clutched a small stuffed Dalmatian to her chest, repeating, "I want my mother," again and again.

As Rosen absorbed the unbelievable tale, all that kept going through his mind was, *It can't be true. Not in Sandy Hook. Not here. Not in Sandy Hook.* Sandy Hook Elementary had always been a place of joy for him. It was where he took his daughter to use the swings. The parking lot was where he had taught his eight-year-old grandson how to ride his bike. The school was only a stone's throw from his house, and seeing the children come every morning had always been a joyous experience for Rosen.

As much as he didn't want to believe their words were true, as the children spoke he remembered he had heard strange noises coming from the school about fifteen minutes earlier. He had heard the sound of gunfire but dismissed it as an obnoxious hunter in the nearby woods or perhaps fireworks. Now he was reconsidering. *Could that sound have been the gunshots the children were talking about?* he thought, before dismissing the notion, refusing to allow the concept to gel in his mind. *No. It can't be true. Not at Sandy Hook. It can't be true.*

It was too much to process right now. His only job at this moment, he told himself, was to provide comfort for these children until their parents arrived.

Susan Ludwig immediately rushed to the school where she saw two police cars outside. She ran to the front door and tried to get in, but a local police officer turned her away.

"My daughter is inside," she told the officer.

"No one is allowed in," he replied.

As she nervously retreated to the parking lot to wait for her daughter, she saw another officer emerge from the building; it was Chapman. He was walking out of the front entrance cradling the body of a young girl in his arms. *Oh my God, that's my child,* was her first thought as she looked at the girl's long brown hair from a distance.

At second glance she felt equal parts terror and relief as she realized it wasn't her daughter but her daughter's friend Olivia Engel. The little girl's body was limp and she was bleeding from her head. Chapman screamed for an ambulance.

A moment later, a second child walked out escorted by another officer. Ludwig couldn't believe the sight as she looked at the little girl, who was covered from head to toe in blood, with pieces of flesh hanging off her body, and watched as she ran to the arms of her mother, in the parking lot.

Ludwig immediately suspected the worst as one by one police cars began filling up the parking lot. *This isn't just a shooting,* she thought. *This is a massacre.*

At 10:05 A.M. an automated voice mail was sent out from the superintendent's office directly to the cell phones of the entire Sandy Hook Elementary parent community telling them that there would be no midday bus run and that afternoon kindergarten was canceled.

A few minutes later, the students began pouring out of the school in single-file lines. Barbara Sibley waited and waited, looking for her son. Finally, after seven classes came out of the building, she spotted him being led by his teacher, Teri Alves. Some of the children were giggling. Others were crying. Her son Daniel had a flat affect. Inside she was falling apart, but as she slowly approached her son as he was being led out through the parking lot, she kept a calm facade.

"Hi, Mom," the little boy said. "What are you doing here?"

"I just happened to be here," she responded.

"Well, we are all going to the firehouse. Do you want to come?"

Two little girls, one in front of him and one behind, were both crying. Barbara put her arms around all three as they walked to the firehouse together in a group hug.

Jillian Soto was at a Vermont ski slope when her cell phone rang at 10 A.M. It was her mother, Donna, reporting that there had been a shooting at Sandy Hook Elementary and the school was under lockdown. Jillian's heart sank. Her big sister, Victoria, was a first-grade teacher at the school.

Forty-five minutes later, a second call came from her mother. The school had been completely evacuated and Vicki had not come out.

"Does that mean Vicki is dead?" asked Jillian.

"No," her mother responded.

Soto and her friends packed the car and began the grueling seven-hour trip back to the family's home in Stratford, Connecticut.

At 11:17 A.M. a third voice mail from the superintendent's office hit the phones of parents: "Parents of Sandy Hook Elementary should pick up your child/children from the firehouse. All other schools remain in lockdown."

CHAPTER 11

———◁◦▷———

FOG OF WAR

The morning of December 14 began as a day of celebration for staff at the *Newtown Bee*. It had just closed its latest weekly edition, which included a front-page report on how well Newtown schools were meeting state standards, when they discovered one of their employees had won a radio contest. News of the award, a catered Christmas party for the entire office, sparked shouts of joy from inside the small red clapboard house that served as the *Bee* headquarters.

Then at 9:35:53 A.M. a short blurb came across the police scanner in the *Bee* office.

"Six-seven. Sandy Hook School, caller's indicated she thinks someone is shooting in the building," the dispatcher deadpanned.

A staffer heard the dispatch and alerted Shannon Hicks, an associate editor, who walked to the back of the office toward the scanner in time to hear the next dispatch twenty-two seconds later:

"The individual I have on the phone is continuing to hear what he believes to be gunshots."

Hicks grabbed her camera and jumped into her 2006 Jeep Wrangler. The school was located only a mile and a quarter from the newspaper's offices. As Hicks pulled onto Riverside Road, she quickly found herself behind a dozen police officers all racing toward Dickinson Drive at full speed, sirens blaring.

A shooting at Sandy Hook? It just seemed too difficult to fathom. It just wasn't the kind of place where school shootings happened. *It must be a domestic dispute*, assumed Hicks as she followed the speeding caravan of emergency vehicles.

Over the course of its 135-year history, the *Bee* has written hundreds of articles about Sandy Hook Elementary School, noting exceptional teachers and chronicling the honor roll activities of the student body. Owned by the same family since it was founded in 1877, the oversize paper's staff of eight reporters and editors takes pride in its hyperlocal coverage, which circulates to about two-thirds of the community.

One popular refrain in the office, that no story is too small to cover, is a motto put to practice across the pages of every issue. The happenings at Sandy Hook Elementary School, no matter how trivial, are always fodder for coverage at the *Bee*.

As she pulled down Dickinson Drive, with one hand on the steering wheel, Hicks began taking photographs through the windshield of her car. A moment after pulling up near the school, she saw Officer Chapman emerge from the front entrance, cradling a bleeding little girl in his arms as he screamed: "Get the bus!"

The twenty-plus-year veteran journalist tried to stay focused, composing each image through the eyepiece of her camera. She aimed her lens and pushed down on the shutter. Hicks, who also serves as a volunteer at Sandy Hook Volunteer Fire & Rescue, then cried out for help. "We need an ambulance," she screamed.

As she looked down to study the image on her camera, she realized it was a photograph that would never see print.

The ambulance pulled up to the entrance. As Officer Chapman approached, he lost his strength and fell to the ground. Several first responders sprang to his aid, picked him up off the ground by his shoulders, and carried the little girl's lifeless body into the ambulance before racing away with lights blaring.

The scene quickly descended into further chaos. A line of fourteen anguished children, their hands on their classmates' shoulders, their eyes closed tightly, was being led out of the school with a teacher in front, a teacher in back, and police at both sides. Looks of horror spread across their faces. Then a second class was evacuated. More children walking single file with hands on each other's shoulders. Eyes closed. They were talking about the wild animal that had gotten loose inside the school. Followed by parents rushing in from all directions. A police officer holding his rifle tight to his chest was standing near the school's entrance, ordering parents to stay back. As they stood outside the front entrance, many began yelling for their children by name.

"What kind of person would do something like this?" a young man standing outside the school began screaming.

A Connecticut State Trooper got out of his car, put on his flak jacket, and announced loudly, "This scene is not secure."

Another reporter from the *Newtown Bee* had shown up. Shannon Hicks handed him the memory card out of her camera, which had all of her images on it, retrieved her Sandy Hook volunteer firefighter uniform, got dressed, and began helping other volunteers set up a triage area near the baseball field to treat the casualties they expected to soon come out of the school.

It started out as a breaking news alert at 10:30 A.M.

The first page from CNN read: "Connecticut State Police are responding to reports of a shooting at a Newtown elementary school in southwestern Connecticut, according to police spokesman Lt. Paul Vance."

The *Hartford Courant* and the *Stamford Advocate,* along with a CNN live truck and several local print and television media were en route. Seventeen minutes later an alert splashed on the computer screens of editors around the country. The link led to a short story posted by the wire services:

NEWTOWN, Conn. - Connecticut State Police say they are assisting local police in Newtown amid reports of a shooting at an elementary school.

The shooting was reported at Sandy Hook Elementary School in Newtown, in western Connecticut.

The *Hartford Courant* reports there are multiple injuries and unconfirmed reports that one of the shooters is dead while the other is still at large.

The school superintendent's office says the district has

locked down schools to ensure the safety of students and staff.

State police spokesman Lt. Paul Vance says they have a number of personnel on the scene to assist.

Multiple injuries? Two shooters? Inside an elementary school in a small upper-middle-class town? There were still few details, but it was enough for editors to justify deploying resources. A steady caravan of reporters, photographers, and television trucks were immediately dispatched from New York City.

Meanwhile, the seven fire trucks at the Sandy Hook volunteer firehouse were cleared from their garages to make room for the scores of children being marched along the four-hundred-foot path from the elementary school. John Voket, the *Bee*'s government reporter, was inside. He went as a reporter, but soon after realizing the scope of the tragedy, focused instead on trying to help in any way he could. As he walked around, trying to get a handle on the situation, concerned parents were calling him on his cell phone, giving descriptions of their children in hopes that he could help find them amid the chaos.

The CNN News blog began churning out minute-by-minute updates from Sandy Hook, streaming out the information to its 36,000 followers on Twitter, and 79,000 on Facebook in real time. The updates hit the mobile devices of editors at news services across the country.

10:53 A.M. Sandy Hook school is on lockdown and students are now being evacuated, a Newtown police spokesman tells us.

11:03 A.M. We're still getting details in of how many people may have been hurt.

11:10 A.M. Details are still really sketchy, but we now have a photo from the Newtown Bee *of children being led from the scene.*

11:27 A.M. The Hartford Courant *citing police, said an unspecified number of people had been shot. The nature of their injuries was unclear, the newspaper said. But it cited police in saying one person had "numerous gunshot wounds."*

Like most people around the country, Ryan Lanza was closely following breaking news of the tragedy coming out of his hometown as it was unfolding. Sitting behind his desk at Ernst & Young, he stared up at the images being broadcast by CNN on a small television above him, seemingly fixated on the screen. Ryan had started at the financial company in 2008, following in his father's footsteps in the tax practice. During his time there he had earned a reputation as a diligent worker and was popular with his coworkers.

This morning, as he stared at the screen, a coworker noticed he wasn't his usual affable self.

"Aren't you from there?" a coworker asked.

Ryan nodded his head, and in a hushed voice said, "That's where I went to school."

• • •

As the morning progressed, CNN's reporters remained head and shoulders ahead of the other news outlets, pushing out new details on its blog.

11:34 A.M. The shooter is dead, a source with knowledge of the investigation tells CNN's Susan Candiotti. Police have recovered two weapons from him, the source added.

11:45 A.M. At least three people were wounded and are in "very serious" condition at a hospital in Danbury, Conn., that town's mayor, Mark Boughton told CNN. He couldn't say whether the victims were children. It's not known whether police killed the alleged shooter or he took his own life. The source says one weapon recovered is a Glock and the other is a Sig Sauer.

12:02 P.M. Multiple local media are reporting there are fatalities. We're checking.

By 12:37 A.M. the CNN news crew had arrived at the scene and found a young third-grade student whose parents agreed to allow her to be interviewed.

"Was everyone crying, scared, and wanting their parents to come get them?" the anchor asked the young student.

As they spoke, the screamer across the bottom of the screen read, "Breaking News: Shooting at Elementary School. Mayor: at least three victims at hospital; condition 'very serious.' "

"Yeah, they were, and then some people were even, like, it sounded like they had a stomachache," the young girl answered.

12:48 P.M. "Close to 20" people have been killed, including at least 10 children, a law enforcement source with knowledge of the investigation says.

Law enforcement had initially leaked the name Ryan Lanza to several reporters, including one at the *Stamford Advocate*, shortly before 1 P.M. A reporter was sent to the brick ranch house on Bartina Lane in the high-end section of Stamford to confirm. The reporter, Maggie Gordon, knew she was at the right address when she saw the police arrive. They knocked on the door, waited a few minutes, and left.

A moment after the police left, shortly after 1:30 P.M., a blue Mini Cooper pulled into the driveway. It was Peter Lanza. He saw the young reporter standing on his property and rolled down his window. "Is there something I can do for you?" he asked politely.

"I am a reporter for the *Stamford Advocate*," Maggie informed him, waiting for a moment of recognition that never came. "I'd been told someone at this address was connected to the shootings in Newtown."

According to the reporter's account in the *Stamford Advocate*:

His expression twisted from patient, to surprise to horror; it was obvious that this moment, shortly after 1:30 P.M. Friday, was the first time he had considered his family could have been involved. He quickly declined to comment, rolled up the window, parked in the right side of the two-car garage and closed the door.

Moments later the reporter could see him sitting at a table in the front of his three-bedroom house, a phone to his left ear and a palm to his right cheek.

More from CNN:

1:51 P.M. The death toll is closer to 30 than 20, a federal law enforcement source in Washington told CNN's John King. Most of those killed are children, the source said.

1:57 P.M. We have just learned that the suspected shooter is 20 years old, a law enforcement source with knowledge of the investigation tells CNN's Susan Candiotti.

2:11 P.M. CNN's Susan Candiotti has just reported that a law enforcement official tells her the suspect is named Ryan Lanza and he is in his 20s.

Ryan Lanza, still sitting at his desk in Times Square, realized he was being accused of mass murder at the same moment that the rest of the world did. He told his boss he needed to leave immediately, offering no explanation, and walked out of his office building and began pleading his innocence through social media.

Ten minutes after CNN identified the shooter as Ryan Lanza, Fox News followed, and four minutes after that it was all over MSNBC. As soon as the name emerged, reporters and producers around the country went straight to social media. On Ryan Lanza's Facebook profile page it appeared that they had found the perfect match, straight out of central casting. Ryan's profile showed a young white male in his twenties dressed in black and wearing aviator sun-glasses, from Newtown, Connecticut, who currently lived in Hobo-ken, New Jersey.

Dozens of news organizations and blogs ran with it in stories and tweets. The picture was on the heavily trafficked Fox News Website. A quick public records search showed that Ryan Lanza lived at 36 Yogananda Street at one point, and he was also listed as living at 1313 Grand Street in Hoboken, New Jersey. Droves of media were immediately deployed in both directions.

On his forty-minute bus ride home, Ryan's phone was blowing up with slurs, accusations, and Facebook friend requests from jour-nalists. He took to social media to defend himself.

"Fuck you CNN it wasn't me," he wrote on his Facebook page as he walked to the train station.

"This is batshit insane," commented his roommate Michael Shapiro. "How the fuck do they jump to such a conclusion with zero evidence?"

The messages continued to flood his phone. Death threats. Others asked for an explanation.

"Everyone shut the fuck up, it wasn't me," he posted three min-utes later.

"Do you need anything ready for you when you get home? Can I set anything out for you to grab and go? Anything else I can do?" posted his roommate Jessica O'Brien.

"I'm on the bus home now, it wasn't me," Ryan responded.

More angry messages accusing him of murder hit his in-box. Thirty minutes after he had left his office, he was getting texts from a coworker telling them that the NYPD had stormed into Ernst & Young looking for him and was raiding his office. Still on his way to Hoboken, he began furiously punching into his phone that he was innocent.

"IT WASN'T ME I WAS AT WORK IT WASN'T ME."

Brett Wilshe, a friend of Ryan Lanza, saw all the commotion on Facebook and sent him a private message.

"What is going on? Is everything all right?"

"The shooter may have had my ID," Ryan messaged back.

A few minutes later, Brett received another message from Ryan. "It was my brother. Oh my God I think my mother is dead."

Despite his pleas of innocence, all the major media networks continued to identify Ryan Lanza as the suspect and reported more erroneous details as they emerged: His mother, Nancy Lanza, was a teacher at the school and had been shot in the classroom; Ryan's brother was found dead in Hoboken.

The CNN blog kept leading the way:

3:09 P.M. The suspect's mother was shot and killed at the school, according to a source close to the investigation. She was a teacher there. And we now know that Ryan Lanza, the suspected gunman, was 24.

3:22 P.M. It appears that another member of the alleged shooter's family is dead. A senior law enforcement official familiar with the investigation says a brother of the alleged shooter was found dead in a home searched in Hoboken, New Jersey. We already knew the suspect's mother was found dead in the elementary school.

3:51 P.M. A federal law enforcement source tells CNN's John King the information from the scene is that the shooter arrived and headed directly toward and to his mother's classroom. That and the other information now emerging— another family member killed, police interviews—lead them to believe his mother was the primary target.

Throughout the afternoon, CNN's Wolf Blitzer began repeating the information about the identity of the gunman over the airwaves. "Just to recap. The shooter in this case, the suspected gunman, identified now as Ryan Lanza. In his twenties. That according to a law enforcement source who told that to CNN. The shooter died at the scene."

Blitzer later added during his 3 P.M. broadcast: "Ryan Lanza's mother, a teacher at this elementary school, was shot and killed herself." Minutes later Blitzer amended his report: "We're also told that the mother of Ryan Lanza, Nancy Lanza, was shot and killed in this classroom, as well as earlier the brother of Ryan Lanza in a residential area of Hoboken, New Jersey."

Shortly before 3 P.M. Ryan Lanza got off the bus in Hoboken, New Jersey, and walked along Grand Street to the five-story brick building known as the Metropolitian.

After a brief few moments inside, Hoboken police arrived, handcuffed him, and led him into a squad car in full view of a CBS television camera. The images were aired across the country. Media outlets quickly scrambled to the Metropolitan, where Hoboken police gathered with FBI agents. As curiosity grew from onlookers and media members, police draped yellow police tape around the perimeter, closing both sides of Grand Street.

Throughout the evening, the police and FBI agents could be seen going in and out of Ryan's apartment as they searched his phone and computer records.

Inside One Police Plaza in Hoboken, Ryan Lanza was being questioned by police. For hours they asked the same questions and Ryan gave the same answers.

"Do you know what your brother has done?" they asked.

Ryan nodded his head and quietly muttered, "Yes."

He had read the news reports on his phone and knew that twenty children were dead. He knew his mother was dead but had still not processed the information. Ryan didn't shed any tears and always referred to his brother as "Adam," and not his brother.

"When was the last time you spoke with Adam?"

"I haven't spoken to him in over a year."

"Do you have any idea why he did this?"

"No," Ryan told them. "I don't know him anymore."

They asked him why the brothers no longer spoke.

"He is sick," he told police. "He didn't talk to anyone."

"Does he have any friends?" they asked.

"I don't think so," Ryan responded.

Law enforcement was satisfied that Ryan had cooperated fully. As he was escorted out of the police station, media swarmed him. He tried to cover his face but couldn't escape the aggressive cameras.

Blitzer continued to report the shooter's name as Ryan Lanza until 5:45 P.M. when the anchor went to the airwaves and corrected himself, saying, "I want to clarify what we earlier, like other news organizations, were reporting that the suspected shooter was Ryan Lanza, age twenty-four. We now believe the shooter was not Ryan Lanza. Ryan Lanza was taken into custody, we're told, earlier in the day."

According to the Associated Press, "a law enforcement official mistakenly transposed the brothers' first names." Soon after, a new report hit the wires. A law enforcement official told the Associated Press that Adam Lanza's girlfriend and another friend were now missing in New Jersey.

Nine hours after Adam Lanza walked into Sandy Hook Elementary School, reliable information remained elusive. There was still little known about the mysterious gunman, and much of what had been reported would later turn out to be wrong.

By nightfall more than two hundred reporters from around the world had descended on the small town and settled on a single horrifying narrative: twenty-six dead, including twenty children and the school principal. The shooter, a twenty-year-old named Adam Lanza, shot his mother at her home, then drove to Sandy Hook Elementary where he murdered the employees and children before committing suicide inside the school.

The media contingent took over the small Sandy Hook downtown area at the intersection of Church Hill Road and Glen, and then spread out across the area in a desperate search for any information that could answer the questions the world was asking:

Who was Adam Lanza? Why did he do this?

CHAPTER 12

———◄o►———

TWENTY-SIX DEAD

By 10:20 A.M. Friday morning, the Sandy Hook volunteer firehouse had already been converted into a makeshift staging area for children, parents, and first responders. Large tarps were spread out across the floor and folding chairs were opened. Bottles of water, bags of chips, and boxes of crackers were being laid out on tables by the Ladies Auxiliary of Sandy Hook. The sounds of cartoons playing could be heard in the background. On another table were plates and pans of pizza donated from My Place Pizza & Restaurant, but no one touched them.

Hundreds of students who had been led safely out of the school were now lined up single file behind their teachers. Sitting in one of the chairs was third-grade teacher Teri Alves. She had become dehydrated and was hyperventilating. Parents began rushing bottles of water to her as quickly as they could move.

Not far away sat kindergarten aide Deborah Pisani, who was

holding a large bandage over the part of her foot where the ricochet bullet had struck. In another area, folding chairs were set up in a circle for an impromptu multifaith service where people began to gather, hold hands, and pray.

At one point a tall man wearing a trench coat had gotten inside and begun taking pictures. Several men tackled him to the ground and held him until two officers made their way over and took him outside and questioned him before ordering him off the property.

Amid the tears of joy, there was a small group of parents who couldn't find their children. They were walking in desperate circles, making cell phone calls, asking anyone for information on where they could go to retrieve their loved ones.

Up the road two officers were stationed next to a wooden barricade set up to block access on Dickinson Drive and direct parents to the firehouse. But some of the parents who had been unable to find their children at the firehouse began trying desperately to get into the school to locate their kids.

"I want to see my child," they screamed.

"At the firehouse you will receive further instructions on how to locate your children," the officers kept repeating patiently.

As more students were reunited with their parents, it soon became apparent that there were two classrooms "unaccounted for," those of Victoria Soto and Amanda D'Amato. Carlee Soto had rushed to Sandy Hook Elementary School as soon as she heard there was a shooting. Shortly after pulling up, she was told her sister Vicki had likely been killed inside. She pressed her left hand to her heart and her face contorted in anguish as she began crying into her cell phone.

An hour away, sitting in traffic, Jillian Soto was with her boyfriend and two other friends, still waiting for an update on her sister Victoria, when she received a phone call from her younger sister, Carlee, telling her that the family was leaving the firehouse and heading home.

"Oh, we know where Vicki is?" said Jillian, her voice full of hope.

"No, we still don't, but Mommy is too tired of sitting here. She just wants to go home," Carlee replied.

The family had already gotten the bad news that Victoria was gone, but they wanted to deliver it to Jillian in person. Moments later Jillian started receiving Facebook messages popping up on the screen of her iPhone from friends offering their condolences.

"I'm so sorry," read one.

"Your sister was a hero," read another.

She called her father. "Tell me what's going on?" she demanded.

"Everything's okay, baby," her father calmly responded. "Just get home. Just drive home. Drive safely. Where are you?"

"I'm in Hartford, stuck in traffic."

"It's fine. Just take your time, get home, and we'll see you when you get here."

"Tell me what's going on!"

Her father told her they were 99 percent sure that Victoria had been killed inside Sandy Hook. He was waiting to identify the body.

Jillian began sobbing. She looked over at her boyfriend, who was in tears.

Becky Kowalski had been waiting by her phone, as instructed, for more information on her son Chase when finally the phone rang.

The caller informed her that they had evacuated the children from the school and that she should go there to pick up her son.

After she arrived at the school, Becky saw a mix of intense emotions. She saw her friends with their children, hugging and rejoicing before taking them home, while other parents had looks of terror etched on their faces as they wandered aimlessly, desperate for information.

"Did you see Chase? Did anyone see Chase?" she began asking, more and more frantically.

"I'm sure he's fine," they kept responding. "Go to the firehouse."

Finally, she spotted another friend who provided her with the answer she had been looking for. "I think I saw Chase with a group of kids outside the school," the friend told her.

On the short drive from the school to the firehouse, she turned on the radio and the news that came through the speakers was unthinkable. There were twenty dead children. Her fears were amplified when, before entering the firehouse, a state trooper told her that the parents of students in her son's class should wait in a special room in the rear of the building. The trooper had her sign a sheet of paper. She counted the signatures. There were twenty.

Outside the school, Scarlett Lewis was looking for her son Jesse. She kept witnessing emotional reunions between parents and children as she waited amid the chaos for her own child. Still, there was no sign of him.

"They took him to the Children's Adventure Center," a parent told her. She ran to the center, near the school, but Jesse wasn't there.

"Oh, I think they took Jesse to the house next door with six other kids," another concerned parent advised.

A couple of hours after the last child had left his house, a knock came on Gene Rosen's door. It was Scarlett. She explained that she was looking for her little boy Jesse.

"I heard there were six children here." The pretty woman's face looked frozen in terror, almost distorted, as she spoke. "Is Jesse Lewis here?"

Rosen looked at the pained woman, knowing he could provide no words of comfort. "No he's not, but let's go to the firehouse," he told her, knowing that she had already been there. Rosen accompanied her on the short walk back to where the grieving families continued to frantically pace.

By 1 P.M. nearly four hours had passed since Adam Lanza had set foot inside Sandy Hook Elementary School. The mood in the firehouse had changed. Gone were the joyous parent-child reunions. The room was filled with only twenty-eight families waiting to hear news of their missing loved ones.

Krista Halstead was convinced that her school secretary mother, Barbara, was dead.

"There is nobody left alive inside," an officer told Krista. "We have checked every nook and cranny."

But unbeknownst to the family or law enforcement, Barbara and school nurse Sally Cox were still hiding in the first-aid closet.

Shortly after 11:15 A.M., almost two hours after the shooting, they decided to open the door a crack. From the slit in their office window they could see several men in the courtyard wearing fatigues and toting weapons, but not knowing whether they were SWAT team members or the attackers they decided to remain hidden. Meanwhile, only feet away in the Principal's office, law enforcement officials had set up their command center.

Neither had cell phones with them but they could hear helicopters overhead and people on the roof of the school shouting and yelling. At one point, someone jiggled the office door, but did not call out.

Finally, at 1:15 P.M., the two women summoned the courage to open the office door. They saw the police, who acted surprised before immediately taking them to safety.

"Close your eyes," the police said as they escorted Barbara and Sally outside.

They reunited with their families. It would be the last moment of joy that day.

In the back room of the old brick firehouse, twenty-six families were asked to sit down. Connecticut governor Dan Malloy walked into the room, standing at his side were local politicians and community leaders, including Newtown First Selectman Patricia Llodra and St. Rose of Lima pastor Robert Weiss. There was no protocol for a situation like this. The traditional routine of having relatives identify a body before confirming death would leave the families waiting for several more hours. The governor made the decision that they had already waited long enough.

He whispered to one of his staffers, "I am not going to take any questions from families of the dead kids." Then he began to address the room of anxious parents in a monotone voice: "Two children were brought to Danbury Hospital and expired."

Most in the room had feared the worst but hearing the news sent many into hysterics. Many fell off their chairs and onto the floor. Several parents screamed out in agony. One man yelled out: "Well, where did the other people go? We want to be with our kids."

The governor took a deep breath. "Nobody else was taken to a hospital," he responded.

"So, what are you telling us, they're all dead?" another parent screamed.

"Yes."

The room was in shock. The wails of pain pushed through the walls and out into the parking lot where those within earshot stopped what they were doing and lowered their heads.

Newtown First Selectman Pat Llodra ordered that each family be assigned a police escort as a shield against the media and to work as a liaison to help convey information and answer any questions or concerns.

Some of the parents remained at the firehouse. A few huddled around a television at 3:15 P.M. to watch as President Barack Obama teared up while delivering his statement expressing his shock, grief, and prayers to the victims.

We've endured too many of these tragedies in the past few years. Each time I learn the news I react not as a president but as anybody else would as a parent.

That was especially true today.

I know there's not a parent in America that doesn't feel the same overwhelming grief that I do.

The majority of those who died today were children, beautiful little kids between the ages of five and ten years old. They had their entire lives ahead of them, birthdays, graduations, weddings, kids of their own.

Among the fallen were also teachers—men and women who devoted their lives to helping our children fulfill their dreams. Our hearts are broken today for the parents and grandparents, sisters and brothers of these children and the families of the adults we lost.

Our hearts are broken for the parents of the survivors as well, for as blessed as they are to have their children home tonight, they know that their children's innocence has been torn away from them too early, and there are no words that will ease their pain.

As a country, we have been through this too many times. Whether it's an elementary school in Newtown, or a shopping mall in Oregon, or a temple in Wisconsin, or a movie theater in Aurora, or a street corner in Chicago—these neighborhoods are our neighborhoods, and these children are our children. And we're going to have to come together and take meaningful action to prevent more tragedies like this, regardless of the politics.

This evening Michelle and I will do what every parent in America will do—hug our children a little tighter and tell them that we love them. There are families in Connecticut that cannot do that tonight and they need all of us tonight.

May God bless the memory of the victims and in the words of Scripture heal the brokenhearted and bind up their wounds.

Governor Dan Malloy left the firehouse to address the media gathered nearby at Treadwell Memorial Park: "Evil visited this community today. And it's too early to speak of recovery, but each parent, each sibling, each member of the family has to understand that Connecticut—we're all in this together. We'll do whatever we can to overcome this event. We will get through it."

Inside the firehouse, Jenny Hubbard had been sitting with Pastor Robert Weiss for several hours waiting for news about her six-year-old daughter, Catherine. Her child was "unaccounted for," she was told. As she waited, she walked around the room trying to comfort the other mothers who were experiencing similar agony.

When the news came that her daughter was gone, her thoughts turned to Catherine's older brother, Freddy. He was only eight. Freddy and Catherine were so close. She turned to her pastor and said, "Father, come with me, and let's tell Freddy."

Together, they gently told the eight-year-old boy of the death of his sister.

The little boy looked back at them and asked, "Who am I going to play with now? I have nobody to play with now."

Barbara Sibley wasn't going to get her car out of the parking lot anytime soon. She and her son Daniel hitched a ride back home with her friend Sandra instead. She draped her suit jacket over her son, whose coat and backpack were still inside the classroom. As she got out of the car she saw her father-in-law, Robert Sibley Sr., waiting in the driveway.

"You've had quite a morning," he said.

Barbara, who had been okay until that moment, collapsed on the driveway, and began crying hysterically. She was having trouble breathing. All she kept repeating was: "I was so afraid."

Her father-in-law helped her into the house where she regained her composure before checking on her twin boys, both of whom were supposed to be going to Sandy Hook Elementary School later that day for afternoon kindergarten.

"We have no school today!" the kids shouted with excitement, before one of them took on a sadder tone when he remembered a sugary treat he would be missing. "Does this mean I can't get my chocolate milk?" he innocently asked.

Daniel walked up the stairs to his room, closed the door behind him, pulled the covers up over his head, and slept the rest of the day.

CHAPTER 13

——◄●►——

HOUSE OF HORRORS

When the tactical team from the Connecticut State Police arrived at 36 Yogananda Street, the address attached to the black Honda Civic, which had been registered to Nancy Lanza, Adam Lanza's body had yet to be positively identified and they were on full alert for an armed conflict. The officers sped up the long driveway and quickly took positions around the exterior. There were no signs of activity inside the home. A large wreath with a red bow hung on the front door and a fresh garland twisted up the columns in front of the entranceway. The driveway was empty, and in the attached garage sat a BMW, idle.

Down the block seventeen more law enforcement vehicles had gathered, blocking off the street. Officers in full riot gear quickly swarmed through the quiet residential upper-middle-class neighborhood, some going from door to door and asking residents to leave their homes. Within seconds of arriving several officers stormed through the front door of the Lanza home, moving quietly from room to room, rifles drawn. The first thing they noticed was that the house was in immaculate order. In the spacious living room, the television was turned off and the remotes were neatly stacked on an end table. In the kitchen, recently watered green plants rested on a sill. There were no dirty dishes in the sink. The team of officers began fanning out in different directions, searching throughout the house.

As they entered the basement, they saw military posters lining the walls and video games stacked neatly in rows not far from a large television screen. The windows had been darkened with shades to prevent sunlight from coming through.

They entered the two upstairs bedrooms belonging to Adam. In the room where his bed was located, they found journals and drawings. They found the covers on his bed neatly laid out and five matching tan colored shirts along with five pairs of khaki pants in his closet. In his other room, which he shared with his mother, investigators found his computers. The hard drives had been destroyed and the internal discs that stored the data scratched. An empty cereal bowl rested nearby. Again, room darkeners covered the windows. Adam had duct-taped black garbage bags over the windows to prevent any light from getting through.

In the upstairs master bedroom they found the remains of a woman. She was in her pajamas, lying on her back. The shades were still drawn. The four gunshot wounds to her head had nearly decapitated her. The wounds suggested the weapon had been pressed directly against her head when fired. At the foot of the bed lay a

Savage Mark .22-caliber rifle with three live rounds inside and one spent cartridge.

As investigators began to sort through the home for clues, it soon became clear that the massacre wasn't a spontaneous act of violence or a momentary break from reality but the result of a tremendous amount of planning and preparation. It had been years in the making.

Most disturbingly, they found a gruesome list of the top five hundred mass murderers in world history. The massive spreadsheet, seven feet long and four feet wide, had ranked the killers in order from most kills to least, along with the precise make and model of the weapons used, all typed out in a tiny nine-point font. The carefully researched document appeared to have taken years to create.

Along with the spreadsheet, investigators discovered newspaper clippings and printed-out articles showing that the killer had created a virtual who's who of mass-murder infamy. Several killers Adam gave particular interest to according to investigators included:

• James Holmes, who killed twelve and wounded fifty-eight moviegoers in an Aurora, Colorado, movie theater in June of 2012.

Holmes parked his car near the exit door of the theater, changed into black clothing, and suited up in military gear preparing for a bloodbath. He put on a gas mask, a load-bearing vest, a ballistic helmet, bullet-resistant leggings, a throat protector, a groin protector, and tactical gloves, and carried a 12-gauge Remington 870 Express Tactical shotgun, and a Smith & Wesson M&P semiautomatic rifle with a hundred-pound drum magazine before walking inside the theater and unloading on the audience.

Holmes fired off seventy rounds, many of which hit multiple people, and was only prevented from shooting more because his rifle jammed. He was apprehended by police outside the theater.

• Charles Carl Roberts IV, who murdered five Amish girls and injured five others inside a one-room Amish schoolhouse in Nickel Mines, Pennsylvania, on October 2, 2006.

Roberts was armed with a handgun, shotgun, rifle, stun gun, two knives, and six hundred rounds of ammunition when he barricaded himself in the schoolhouse along with twenty-eight other people. The deranged gunman ordered the hostages, most of them children, to line up against the chalkboard and then released all but ten female students.

Roberts fired at least thirteen rounds from his 9-millimeter semiautomatic pistol, shooting five girls, between the ages of six and thirteen, in the head execution style, before killing himself.

• Steven P. Kazmierczak, who shot twenty-one people, killing five, at Northern Illinois University on February 14, 2008.

Kazmierczak walked into Cole Hall wearing dark

brown boots, jeans, and a black T-shirt reading TERRORIST, imposed over an image of a rifle. His arsenal included three handguns, a 9-millimeter Glock 19, a 9-millimeter Kurz Sig Sauer P232, and a .380 Hi-Point CF380; a 12-gauge Remington Sportsman 48 shotgun concealed in a guitar case; eight loaded magazines; and a knife.

He walked up and down the aisle, firing fifty-four shots into the lecture hall as students scrambled for the exits. Kazmierczak turned the gun on himself before police were able to arrive.

• Jared Loughner, who shot eighteen people, killing twelve, and severely injuring Congresswoman Gabrielle Giffords at a constituents' meeting in a grocery store parking lot in Tucson, Arizona, on January 8, 2011.

Loughner walked into the "Congress at Your Corner" event sponsored by the congresswoman armed with a 9-millimeter Glock 19 pistol with a 33-round magazine before he opened fire on Giffords from close range, as well as numerous bystanders, including a nine-year-old girl.

Loughner was tackled by bystanders as he tried to flee the scene.

• John Allen Muhammad and Lee Boyd Malvo, who killed ten people and wounded three others in Washington, D.C., Maryland, and Virginia during their October 2002 terror spree.

Over the course of twenty-three days, ten people were randomly gunned down by a Bushmaster .223-caliber rifle while doing random everyday tasks such as reading a book, mowing the lawn, shopping, or pumping gas.

After an exhaustive manhunt, both were later apprehended by law enforcement.

Still, of all the mass killers Adam studied, investigators believed it was the name on the top of his list of killers, the Norwegian gunman Anders Behring Breivik, who proved the most influential. Over the course of his research on mass killers, it was believed that Adam had become obsessed with Breivik's killing spree in July 2011.

"We believe Adam studied him closely and may have tried to imitate some of his techniques," said one official familiar with the investigation. "They both used the same video games to train and prepare and they were both obsessed with other mass killers."

After setting off a series of bombs in downtown Oslo that killed eight people, Breivik made his way to Utøya Island where, dressed as a police officer and carrying an arsenal of weapons, he systematically hunted down and shot dead sixty-nine others, most of them young people attending a summer camp. When an armed police SWAT unit from Oslo arrived on the island and confronted him, he surrendered without resistance.

Breivik left behind a fifteen-hundred page manifesto, "2083: A European Declaration of Independence." In the pages, Adam found detailed instructions on how to prepare for the solitary journey and eventual gratification that encompassed one's preparations for a mass killing. Investigators believed Adam may have been able to relate to Breivik, who thought of himself as a loner on a one-man crusade to educate the world through his destructive means.

Breivik wrote: "You are normally required to plan absolutely everything alone; fight alone to see your mission through and you are likely to die alone with half of your city's system protectors hunting you. However, I have never in my life felt that I have done anything more meaningful than what I am doing now regardless of the lack of moral support from my founding brothers or other armed resistance fighters. Support from our extremely distributed and anonymous 'non-hierarchy' out there would be nice but I have managed to cope through mental discipline to become what I am today; a self-driven and highly effective manifestation of an independent resistance cell. I have managed to stay focused and highly motivated for a duration of more than 9 years now. I feel really happy about my current course."

Investigators also turned up evidence that led them to believe that Adam, like Breivik, used his violent video games to prepare for his killing spree. In the video game *Call of Duty, Modern Warfare 2,* Breivik believed he had found the perfect tool to hone his killing skills.

"I just bought *Modern Warfare 2,* the game. It is probably the best military simulator out there and it's one of the hottest games this year," wrote Breivik. "I see *MW2* more as a part of my training-simulation than anything else. I've still learned to love it though and especially the multiplayer part is amazing. You can more or less completely simulate actual operations."

At the subsequent trial, Breivik expanded on the video game's usefulness in his preparations for the slaughter. The thirty-three-year-old said he practiced his shot using a "holographic aiming device" on the war-simulation game, which he said is used by armies around the world for training.

"You develop target acquisition," he said. "It consists of many hundreds of different tasks and some of these tasks can be compared with an attack, for real. That's why it's used by many armies throughout the world. It's very good for acquiring experience related to sights systems."

Breivik added: "If you are familiar with a holographic sight, it's built up in such a way that you could have given it to your grandmother and she would have been a super marksman. It's designed to be used by anyone. In reality it requires very little training to use it in an optimal way. But of course it does help if you've practiced using a simulator."

Inside the Lanza's Colonial-style home investigators also discovered a stockpile of disparate weaponry: several firearms, ammunition, and knives, along with macabre pictures. In addition to the rifle found at the foot of Nancy's bed, investigators also discovered an Enfield bolt-action rifle, a WW II–era rifle long obsolete for military purposes because of its slow rate of fire; another rifle; a BB gun; a starter pistol; and 1,600 rounds of ammunition scattered around the house, some of them housed in a Planters peanut can and a Nike shoe box in different closet spaces. There was no sign that the gun locker, which was open when investigators arrived, had been broken into or tampered with.

Along with the firearms, they also discovered a cache of bladed weapons inside the house, including a Panther brand brown-handled folding knife with a 3.75-inch blade, a 6-foot 10-inch wood-handled two-sided pole with a blade on one side and a spear on the opposite side, a samurai sword with a canvas-wrapped handle and a 28-inch blade with a sheath, a samurai sword with a canvas-wrapped handle and a 21-inch blade with a sheath, and a samurai sword with a canvas-wrapped handle and a 13-inch blade with a sheath.

As they sorted through Adam's belongings in his upstairs bedrooms, they made several more disturbing discoveries. A photograph of Adam holding a gun to his head along with three photographs of what appeared to be dead bodies covered in plastic and blood. They also recovered seven personal memoirs; notes and drawings by Adam, several with violent images; a military uniform; and his first-grade report card from Sandy Hook Elementary.

Other items law enforcement bagged as evidence included an NRA certificate for Nancy and Adam Lanza; paper and cardboard targets; school records, medical prescriptions; psychiatric records; and subscriptions, along with a holiday card made out to Adam Lanza from his mother, Nancy, that contained a Bank of America check that specified that the money was to buy a "C183," which investigators believe was for the purchase of a handgun.

Along with all the mass-killer study sheets, violent images, and the weaponry found inside the home, investigators also came across two books, both connected to autism: *Look Me in the Eye: My Life with Asperger's* written by John Elder Robison, a first-person account of a man living with Asperger's who wasn't diagnosed until the age of forty; and *Born on a Blue Day: Inside the Extraordinary*

Mind of an Autistic Savant written by Daniel Tammet, who, according to the publisher, "is virtually unique among people who have severe autistic disorders in that he is capable of living a fully independent life and able to explain what is happening inside his head. He sees numbers as shapes, colors, and textures, and he can perform extraordinary calculations in his head. He can learn to speak new languages fluently, from scratch, in a week. In 2004, he memorized and recited more than 22,000 digits of pi, setting a record. He has savant syndrome, an extremely rare condition that gives him the most unimaginable mental powers, much like those portrayed by Dustin Hoffman in the film *Rain Man.*"

A third book, *Train Your Brain to Get Happy,* had pages tabbed off and the subtitle promised readers "joy, optimism, and serenity."

CHAPTER 14

———◄◊►———

THE THREE DAYS AFTER

At 8:37 P.M. on December 17, President Barack Obama stepped up to the podium at the Newtown High School auditorium—the same stage where only seventy-two hours earlier the fourth-graders had performed the Winter Concert—in an attempt to provide comfort for a community and nation still searching for answers.

"We gather here in memory of twenty beautiful children and six remarkable adults. They lost their lives in a school that could have been any school; in a quiet town full of good and decent people that could be any town in America," the president began.

The room was packed. A hundred more crowded near speakers in the school's gym, while others huddled outside in a cold drizzle, holding candles and weeping at times. The president went on to speak of the acts of bravery and heroism from the teachers and first responders and of how the community had pulled together as one during these trying times before making a broader call on the country as a whole to meet our collective obligation to protect our children.

And by that measure, can we truly say, as a nation, that we are meeting our obligations? Can we honestly say that we're doing enough to keep our children—all of them—safe from harm? Can we claim, as a nation, that we're all together there, letting them know that they are loved, and teaching them to love in return? Can we say that we're truly doing enough to give all the children of this country the chance they deserve to live out their lives in happiness and with purpose?

I've been reflecting on this the last few days, and if we're honest with ourselves, the answer is no. We're not doing enough. And we will have to change.

Since I've been president, this is the fourth time we have come together to comfort a grieving community torn apart by a mass shooting. The fourth time we've hugged survivors. The fourth time we've consoled the families of victims. And in between, there have been an endless series of deadly shootings across the country, almost daily reports of victims, many of them children, in small towns and big cities all across America—victims whose, much of the time, their only fault was being in the wrong place at the wrong time.

We can't tolerate this anymore. These tragedies must end. And to end them, we must change. We will be told that the causes of such violence are complex, and that is true. No single law, no set of laws can eliminate evil from the world, or prevent every senseless act of violence in our society.

But that can't be an excuse for inaction. Surely, we can do better than this. If there is even one step we can take to save another child, or another parent, or another town, from the grief that has visited Tucson, and Aurora, and Oak Creek, and Newtown, and communities from Columbine to Blacksburg before that—then surely we have an obligation to try.

He ended the speech by reading the names of the twenty children whose lives were lost. Before leaving the podium to a standing ovation, he added: "Let us make this country worthy of their memory."

In the hour before his speech, the president had gathered inside the school with the families of the victims and first responders. At several points, he became overwhelmed with emotion. His eyes filled with moisture and a single tear trickled down his cheek as he repeatedly offered his prayers.

After meeting with the families, he went to a classroom set up as his staging area where he spotted a message on the whiteboard from Steve George, a Newtown High School teacher and football coach, and Bobby Pattison, a teacher: "The Newtown community is so thankful that you are coming to help us heal," the two teachers had written. "In times of adversity it is reassuring to know that we have a strong leader to help us recover."

The president picked up a marker and wrote, "You're in our thoughts and prayers."

. . .

As Barack Obama left town, many locals began to wish he would take all the tourists and out-of-town media along with him. Tensions were beginning to boil over.

"Go home!" locals could be heard shouting at television trucks or anyone seen holding a notepad.

The Newtown police, still struggling with their own internal trauma from what many of them had witnessed that day, were now in a constant rotation of being dispatched to remove reporters from areas of private property that were being overrun by news crews. The small shops in the Sandy Hook center were particularly affected by this crush of media. For many businesses, the ten days before Christmas were the most important time of the year, possibly making the financial difference between economic life and death, but the stagnant traffic of Church Hill Road kept business away.

Those who waited in the traffic jam to shop in Newtown soon found that all the parking spots had been overtaken by media and curious well-wishers. Inside the hair salons, liquor store, toy store, and antiques shop, merchants waited for customers, but every time the door opened it was another reporter. One local resident's fence was broken by a news truck that just drove on. Some crews left garbage piled near the overflowing trash cans.

The local weekly paper the *Newtown Bee* had seen enough. Since Friday morning, the small-town paper with its deep community roots and wealth of local sources made the decision to abandon the more conventional journalistic mission of bringing the facts of the story to its readership, and instead set its sights on helping the town heal.

On December 17, the *Bee* posted an open plea to fellow journalists on its Facebook page: "On behalf of the entire staff of *The Bee* — we are imploring ALL our colleagues and journalists to PLEASE STAY AWAY FROM THE VICTIMS. We acknowledge it is your right to try and make contact, but we beg you to do what is right and let them grieve and ready their funeral plans in peace."

The post quickly went viral.

Local politicians had also gotten into the act, encouraging the media to leave town. "The story is over. The families are burying their loved ones. Please leave our towns," said State Representative DebraLee Hovey during a capital memorial service.

However, the public's appetite for more information in the wake of the biggest story of the year would prove too much to resist as reporters from all around the world continued to flock to Newtown. The media had also descended on Stamford, Connecticut, where Peter Lanza lived. On Saturday he issued a statement sending his condolences to the families of victims: "Our family is grieving along with all those who have been affected by this enormous tragedy. No words can truly express how heartbroken we are. We are in a state of disbelief and trying to find whatever answers we can."

The media also swooped into the small town of Kingston, New Hampshire, where Adam Lanza was born and where Nancy Lanza had also been born and was raised. Her family released a statement expressing shock and sadness at the tragedy: "On behalf of Nancy's mother and siblings we reach out to the community of Newtown and express our heartfelt sorrow for the incomprehensible and profound loss of innocence that has affected so many."

With the national media spotlight shining on Newtown, sick pranksters saw an opportunity to send shock waves through the grieving community. Dozens of death threats were being called in to the police stations and churches where mourners were seeking solace.

On Sunday night at the rehearsal for the Newtown Christmas pageant that was supposed to memorialize Olivia Engel, a collective gasp went through the packed church when Monsignor Robert Weiss took to the lectern to announce that he needed to evacuate the church.

"We have just been threatened," Father Weiss told the shocked parishioners. "Mass has ended."

Along with those gathered to practice for the pageant, more than four hundred already shattered mourners were forced to evacuate to a nearby chapel because of the depraved caller. Most managed to stay calm during the five-minute evacuation, but some children began crying and asking for comfort and reassurance from their shaken moms and dads.

"Who would do such a thing? It was a real breaking point for me," Weiss recalled.

That was only the beginning of a week of death threats that plagued the small town. Earlier that morning authorities warned that people posing as killer Adam Lanza were posting threatening messages on Facebook and Twitter. Lieutenant Paul Vance of the Connecticut State Police also warned that they "will crack down hard on any jokers who add to Newtown's misery" and were actively searching for the person whose death threats forced the evacuation of a local Catholic church Sunday in the middle of a noontime Mass. "It's not funny. It's not a joke. It's not acceptable for anyone to make any kind of inner threat or statement relative to the security. It's just sick and it won't be tolerated," said an emotional Vance.

The town was on high alert, looking at any out-of-place box or outsider with suspicion. Reports of a man dressed in black carrying a gun in the nearby town of Ridgefield sparked a police mobilization—and sent chills down the spines of many in Newtown.

"The gun turned out to be an umbrella," said Captain Tom Comstock of the Ridgefield police. "A lot of people are on edge, just because of Friday."

In Newtown, it appeared that the families wouldn't even be able to bury their loved ones in peace.

———⟨◦⟩———

CHAPTER 15

TWENTY-SIX FUNERALS

Colorful holiday decorations of red and green had disappeared and been replaced by somber black bunting. One by one by one by one, hearses crisscrossed the narrow streets of Newtown and its neighboring communities in a seemingly never-ending series of funeral processions.

MONDAY:

Noah Pozner and Jack Pinto

The first two funerals happened on Monday. Two students who sat three desks apart in Lauren Rousseau's class, Noah Pozner and Jack Pinto, were laid to rest within hours of each other. It would become an all too familiar routine that stretched out over the next six days.

As little Noah Pozner was buried, security was tight. Death

threats were coming from all around. Law enforcement didn't believe any were credible but weren't about to take any chances. A total of thirty local police officers along with several additional cops from the Connecticut State Police were assigned to the service to look for anything out of the ordinary. Nearby parking lots, the grounds, and even the flowers sent to the home were carefully checked and double-checked by local law enforcement for irregularities.

Inside the Abraham L. Green and Son Funeral Home in Fairfield, Connecticut, all eyes were on Veronique Pozner, whose beautiful eulogy to the overflowing crowd celebrating her six-year-old son Noah's imprint on the world moved many to tears.

"It's a sad, sad day, and it's also your day, Noah, my little man," she said.

I will miss your forceful and purposeful little steps stomping through our house. I will miss your perpetual smile. The twinkle in your dark blue eyes framed by eyelashes that would be the envy of any lady in this room. Most of all, I will miss your visions of your future. You wanted to be a doctor, a soldier, and a taco factory manager. It was your favorite food and no doubt you wanted to ensure that the world kept producing tacos.

You are a little boy whose life force had all the gravitational pull of a celestial body. You are light, and love, mischief, and pranks. You adored your family with every fiber of your six-year-old being. We are all of us elevated in our humanity by having known you.

Our little maverick, who didn't always want to do his

homework or clean up his toys but practicing his ninja moves or Super Mario on the Wii seemed far more important.

Noah, you will not pass through this way again. I can only believe that you were planted on earth to bloom in heaven.

Back in Newtown dozens of families who could not fit into the Honan Funeral Home stood outside in the cold and rain, waiting to pay their respects to six-year-old Jack Pinto. The brown-haired first-grader was laid to rest adorned in the number 80 jersey of his favorite player on the New York Giants, Victor Cruz. A small hand-written note was left beside the casket by his playmate John:

You are my best friend. We had fun together. I will miss you. I will talk to you in my prayers. I love you, Jack. Love, John.

Among the personal items tucked inside the coffin to travel with Jack to his final resting place were a small brown wooden cross, a plush blue shark, and a ceramic statue of an angel. Jack's parents, Dean and Tricia Pinto, and both sets of grandparents choked back tears as clergy said prayers. Before leaving for the burial, his weeping parents, with tears streaming down their cheeks, took turns kissing their slain son's forehead.

TUESDAY:

James Mattioli, Jessica Rekos,

Madeline Hsu, and Avielle Richman

On Tuesday there were four more funerals, as families said good-bye to three students from Lauren Rousseau's class: James Mattioli, Jessica Rekos, and Madeline Hsu, along with Victoria Soto's student Avielle Richman.

Inside the St. Rose of Lima church, James Mattioli's mother, Cindy, tearfully spoke in front of the five hundred mourners:

> *. . . I loved watching you, Dad, and Anna watch* America's Funniest Home Videos *and laugh hysterically. I love that you loved school so much. You were a great swimmer, never tiring of the water and I was so proud of you. I love that you loved hamburgers. I do, too.*
>
> *Thank you for being your dad's little helper, thank you for being Anna's best playmate and confidant. Thank you for letting me always curl on the couch with you and have a chat before bed about what we did today and what tomorrow would hold.*
>
> *Thank you for lighting up the world with your smile. James, I want you to know we love you. We love you all.*

The Mattioli funeral was immediately followed by the service for his six-year-old classmate Jessica Rekos inside the same Newtown church. As one set of grief-stricken mourners rapidly filed out, the next group arrived. Jessica, who loved horses, was promised her own pony on her tenth birthday. It was a dream that would forever be unfulfilled. Much like her Christmas presents that would never be opened.

"She wanted cowgirl boots—real cowgirl boots, not ones from Target," her mother, Krista, told the countless sets of people with misty eyes who had come to pay their respects.

And she wanted a cowgirl hat, and it had to be black. Santa was going to bring those things next week.

She was a great big sister. She was teaching Travis how to read . . . when her life was cut short. She was beyond excited when I had Shane in April. She begged for any chance to hold, feed, and play with her baby brother.

Away from the glare of the national spotlight, two private services took place that day. Avielle Richman, known to her family as Avie, was a student in Victoria Soto's class and was also remembered for her love of horses, the Harry Potter books, and the color red. The parents of Madeleine Hsu, a member of Lauren Rousseau's class, said their slain little girl stood out for the affection she had for her two sisters, five-year-old Hannah and eight-year-old Rebecca.

Both were laid to rest at the Lakeview Cemetery in Bridgeport.

WEDNESDAY:

Daniel Barden, Caroline Previdi, Charlotte Bacon, Chase Kowalski, Victoria Soto, and Dawn Hochsprung

Six more services took place on Wednesday—four more students from Lauren Rousseau's class: Daniel Barden, Caroline Previdi, Charlotte Bacon, and Chase Kowalski, as well as the funerals for teacher Victoria Soto and principal Dawn Hochsprung.

Victoria Leigh Soto was laid to rest in a wooden casket covered with white flowers, and to the strains of "The Sounds of Silence" inside the Lordship Community Church in Stratford, Connecticut. Midway through the funeral, singer Paul Simon, who knew the Soto family through his sister-in-law, picked up his acoustic guitar and began to sing the twenty-seven-year-old teacher's favorite song without introduction, as her three siblings, Jillian, Carlee, and brother Carlos, wept. When Simon finished, there was no applause, just a reverent silence.

Mourners spoke of her bravery in trying to protect her students until her last moment of life.

Her sister Jillian shared a letter she had recently received that provided her with comfort:

Somebody wrote me a letter about the recent tragedy that I would like to share with you: In it, it said they had to sit down with three small children, explaining to them that monsters sadly do exist out there. But they felt relief that because of my sister, they were able to tell them that superheroes also are very real.

Jillian looked down at her sister.

You are my superhero.

Back in Newtown, little Daniel Barden was given a firefighter's farewell. Hundreds of fire officials lined the street in a silent show of support, saluting Daniel's coffin. Bagpipers played as the funeral procession approached the St. Rose of Lima Roman Catholic Church from the town's main intersection. Many of the smoke eaters wore green and white ribbons, the Sandy Hook Elementary School colors, in solidarity with the victims.

Daniel Barden would never get the chance to live out his dream of being a New York City firefighter. Mourners entered the church to find framed photos of Daniel as a baby, along with his siblings, on a small wooden table near the altar. His small ivory casket had gold embellishments. A wooden crucifix had been laid on the top.

The family had just picked out their Christmas tree one week earlier, Monsignor Robert Weiss told the massive crowd, before raising the question all of America had been asking: "How could this happen? It was just like any other day. A child goes to school and you expect them to be safe—then in a matter of moments, life changes forever."

The funeral of Caroline Previdi had to be delayed for a few minutes as mourners navigated the heavy traffic and crowds leaving Daniel's funeral after it came to a conclusion. Friends and family leaving

Daniel's Mass walked past those arriving for Caroline's, both at St. Rose of Lima. Some people stayed for both.

Again, Monsignor Robert Weiss stood at the lectern, beginning this time by praising Caroline's contagious affection for life. "This is probably the happiest addition to heaven in a long time," Monsignor Weiss declared to the crowd, most of whom were dressed in pink, the little girl's favorite color. "We have a new saint."

In a pew at the very front, holding it together as best they could, sat Caroline's parents, Jeff and Sandy Previdi, and her older brother. Two full-color blowups of their daughter smiled back at them from where her casket had been placed.

An overflow crowd of seventy people waited outside the church, listening on hastily added speakers. "She will intercede for us; turn to her," Weiss told them all. "We have an angel."

Less than two miles away, Charlotte Bacon was being remembered at Christ the King Lutheran Church for her love of all animals and the color pink. Buttons with an image of the radiant child in full smile were distributed to the mourners. An angel superimposed over the name "Charlotte" was featured on the cover of the funeral program.

Charlotte's aunt Georgie delivered the eulogy, asking that everyone gathered remember the vibrant little girl for the way she lived her life, and not for the tragedy of her death.

My wish today, is that when you think of Charlotte, or when
we speak of her, that we remember a sweet, bright little girl

who loved animals, the color pink, and dresses—not how she was killed.

A statement released to the press by the family described the heartbreak:

Charlotte Helen Bacon is the beloved daughter of Joel and JoAnne Bacon, and the sister of Guy Bacon. Charlotte was an extraordinarily gifted six-year-old who filled her family each day with joy and love. The family will forever remember her beautiful smile, her energy for life, and the unique way she expressed her individuality, usually with the color pink. Charlotte never met an animal she didn't love, and since the age of two wanted to be a veterinarian. She also enjoyed practicing tae kwon do weekly with her dad and brother where she relished kicking and throwing punches!

Charlotte has left a place in her entire extended family's hearts that will never be replaced. The family is profoundly grateful for the thoughts and prayers of the many friends around the world who expressed their sympathies. They trust in the depths of God's grace, and with confidence, know that Charlotte rests in God's arms.

As little Charlotte Bacon's casket was taken to be buried, fourteen miles away at the Spadaccino and Leo P. Gallagher & Son Community Funeral Home in Monroe, Connecticut, seven-year-old Chase Kowalski was being remembered as a "funny little guy" whose smile would "light up the room." Standing over her son's casket, Chase's grieving mother, Becky Kowalski, welcomed visitors with a smile. She still felt numb over a vision of her son she believed she had seen three days earlier.

The grieving mother believed her son had appeared to her to provide strength and comfort in moving forward with advocacy and charitable work. "He came to tell me to explain to my husband that the scope of this event was so large and that there were so many people around the country and the world we were touching," she told New York *Daily News* columnist Denis Hamill. "I felt that my son was here in this vision to tell me that the not-for-profit scholarship organization that we are starting in Chase's honor will save lives, change building codes, demand gun and ammunition control, and that in Chase's name I would like to bring God back to America."

Later that evening in Woodbury, Connecticut, a large American flag hung near the doorway of the Munson Lovetere Funeral Home and small lights spelling out the word "hope" were set up on the lawn out front as mourners, including U.S. Education Secretary Arne Duncan, hailed Sandy Hook principal Dawn Hochsprung as a hero. Hundreds of people waited outside in the frigid night to pay their respects during calling hours for the beloved forty-seven-year-old.

While they waited in the long line to get inside the funeral home, friends, teachers, and former students shared their favorite "Principal Dawn" stories, many about the crazy outfits she wore on theme days or her familiar sayings, none remembered more so than her mantra, "Be kind. It's really all that matters."

THURSDAY:

Lauren Rousseau, Catherine Hubbard, Benjamin Wheeler,
Anne Marie Murphy, Jesse Lewis, and Allison Wyatt

On Thursday the seemingly never-ending march of broken hearts stretched into a grueling fourth day when the community laid to rest six more victims, teacher Lauren Gabrielle Rousseau and two of her students, Catherine Violet Hubbard and Benjamin Andrew Wheeler. Memorial services were also held for teacher's aide Anne Marie Murphy and two more students, Jesse Lewis and Allison Wyatt, both from Victoria Soto's class.

That morning Jesse Lewis's heroic actions, imploring his classmates to "run," were rewarded with a commander-in-chief's funeral outside the Honan Funeral Home in Newtown, an honor usually reserved for heads of state and soldiers who have fallen in the act of valor. The fleet of twenty police cars with their sirens on escorted Jesse's parents, Neil Heslin and Scarlett Lewis, as they followed the hearse on their way to the service with two motorcycles on each side.

Upon entering the service mourners were greeted with a collage of photos; one was of baby Jesse smiling in a bubble bath, another showed him frozen in midtoddle in a pumpkin patch. A handwritten note, placed beside the casket, brought many to tears:

"Thank you, Jesse, for blessing us with your presence if only for a short while," it read in bold black letters. "I look forward to seeing you again." It was signed, "With love, Your Mamma."

Jesse's open casket was lined with GI Joe action figures and at his feet lay a plush white teddy bear wearing a blue T-shirt with the number one on it. In a room off to the side, Jesse's older brother, sporting a navy blue suit, reached his arms up to comfort his mother as she wept.

A mile away a bell tolled at the St. Rose of Lima Roman Catholic Church to commemorate the life of Catherine Violet Hubbard. Several hundred people filed into the church pews; some began sobbing uncontrollably as her grieving mother, Jenny, with her husband, Matt, standing by her side, delivered a heart-wrenching eulogy, remembering their bubbly redheaded daughter as a precocious child who loved animals and her older brother, Freddy.

. . . Catherine loved her brother. He was her Freddy. And whatever he could do, she would surely follow. They always protected each other. When Catherine started Sandy Hook school, she cried. I found out later that Fred was walking her to her classroom, every day, just to make sure that she was okay. He did this after she convinced him that he had to walk her on the first day. She took care of him, too. No matter when he called her, or if she was in the midst of something else, she would put down her crayon, and give us a look, or a sigh, and then she would do it. I don't think that she knew every day her being on the bus assured Freddy that he was on the right one. Freddy asked us the other day: How will I know I'm on my bus if Catherine isn't on it?

*Fred. . . . you will always have your little redhead to pro-
tect you.*

A brief moment of relative lightness came as Monsignor Weiss
spoke from the pulpit directly to her older brother, Freddy. "You said
'I lost my best friend. I lost my best buddy.' That is a big brother. And
you know what? Maybe you won't see her, but she's there. You just
have to look up, and you'll see her. She's going to give you a wink."

"She already did," the proud big brother replied without hesitation, as he held up a coin that President Obama had given him during his visit earlier in the week.

In the neighboring town of Danbury, teacher Lauren Rousseau,
who perished while trying to shepherd Catherine and her other
young students away from the danger, was being remembered for
her passion and the childlike innocence she brought to her job that
made her such a great educator. Dozens of mourners had to be
turned away by fire marshals from the First Congregational Church
on Deer Hill Avenue, which had quickly filled to capacity. Inside,
friends and family shed tears as they remembered the spirited,
good-natured thirty-year-old with the joyous heart.

The service began with the song "Jesus Loves the Little Children" before a family friend read aloud several Scriptures. Many recalled her lifelong desire to be a teacher, and the fulfillment she felt
in finding her "life partner" Tony Lusardi III. "I called her 'busy bee'
and she called me 'worker bee,' " he recalled in an emotional eulogy.

Others remembered the angel smiley-face icon she used when sending instant messages or her infectious laugh that "rose all the way up from her toes." But above all, it was her inner child that stoked the passion she had for her students. According to her father, Gilles Rousseau, "She was like a kid in many ways. That's why she liked working with kids so much."

At the same time in Katonah, New York, another educator was being praised. Anna Marie Murphy, whose body was found draped over little Dylan Hockley in an apparent effort to protect and comfort her pupil during his final moments, was remembered for a full life as a mother of four, and for the selfless final act that had inspired so many.

Cardinal Timothy Dolan, the archbishop of New York, presided over the service at St. Mary of the Assumption Church, and likened the bravery of the fifty-two-year-old mother of four to that of Jesus at her funeral Mass. "I never had the honor of meeting Annie, so I'm at a disadvantage," Cardinal Dolan told mourners.

Then again, I never had the honor of physically meeting Jesus, yet my union with him is the most important thing in my life. And because I know Jesus, I feel as if I know Anne Marie McGowan Murphy quite well.

Like Jesus, Annie was an excellent teacher. Like him, she had a favored place in her big, tender heart for children, especially those with struggles. Like Jesus, Annie laid down her life for her friends. Like Him, she had brought together a community, a nation, a world, now awed by her own life and death.

Back in Newtown, Benjamin Andrew Wheeler was being remembered by friends, family, and dozens of his fellow Scouts from Tiger Scout Den 6 who lined the pathway to Trinity Episcopal Church. Inside the church, on each side of the altar stood illuminated five-foot-tall lighthouses, which were one of the six-year-old's many passions.

Before her sermon, Reverend Kathleen E. Adams-Shepherd had invited all the children present in the church to come sit at the altar with her for a moment where she spoke to them about Ben's love of lighthouses and what it means to discover light in darkness. "When something happens to someone or someone dies, that light does not go out. It doesn't. It shines forever and ever and ever," she told the children as she handed them each wooden ornaments of lighthouses with Ben's name on them before sending them back to their seats.

At the start of the service, his parents, David and Francine, who were performers in New York City before moving to Newtown, played a recording of Francine singing a lullaby they called "Stars in the Sky." A rendition of "Here Comes the Sun" was also played in memory of Benjamin, who was a budding Beatles fan.

In her sermon that followed, Reverend Adams-Shepherd told her parishioners that it was not God's plan to take the children and that Adam should never have had access to the weapons.

This awful, horrible, unfathomable act of violence was not the will of God. Horribly awful actions taken by a young, troubled, afflicted man did this. We need to do something and make sure people like him get the support they need. And I am certain that God weeps, that God wept and weeps with us now. It was not a lack of faith or love, it was not God snatching him from you, taking those innocent, beautiful children and those wonderfully brave adults. It was an enraged and sick young man with access to weapons that should never, ever be in a home.

The congregation erupted in applause.

Nearby, in Southbury, Allison "Allie" Wyatt was being remembered as a funny, vibrant, six-year-old who would share her beloved Goldfish crackers with strangers and cover her family's home with her artistic and optimistic visions of life. A soloist sang "Hallelujah" as two Connecticut state troopers led the devastated family into the Sacred Heart Church, while pallbearers slowly carried the small white casket to the front.

Reverend Walter Pitman led the service, telling parishioners that Allison should be remembered for the undeniable joy within her soul and as a teacher to her sister, Lauren, who she taught how to ride the school bus. "You are a very fortunate group," he told the audience. "At some point over the past six years, Allie Wyatt got in your way and you are better for it."

FRIDAY:

Rachel D'Avino, Mary Sherlach, Grace McDonnell,

Olivia Engel, and Dylan Hockley

On Friday morning the nation paused as the tolling of church bells reverberated throughout Newtown, commemorating one week since the mass shooting at Sandy Hook Elementary School. At 9:30 A.M. bell towers across Connecticut chimed twenty-six times to honor each of the victims. Friday was also another day of funerals. Laid to rest were educator Rachel D'Avino; school psychologist Mary Sherlach; and three students: Grace McDonnell, who was in Lauren Rousseau's class, and two students from Victoria Soto's class, Olivia Engel and Dylan Hockley.

Shortly after the bells tolled, hundreds squeezed into the pews at St. Rose of Lima Roman Catholic Church to say their final good-byes to little Grace McDonnell. Her heartbroken mother stood in front of the packed pews and shared her treasured memories of her slain daughter, confiding that she had a secret bedtime ritual with her precious "fashionista," featuring a several-minute-long hand-shake and ending with them both saying the words "hot fire."

"You made me fearless," said Lynn McDonnell. "We were best friends, soul mates, and 'sister girls,' " she said, placing her daughter's favorite stuffed animal on the lectern.

"Gracie," as her family affectionately called her, also had a love of peace signs. Each day after Grace finished her shower, she always drew small peace signs with her finger through the fog on the bathroom window. On the first day without her daughter, the bathroom fogged up and Lynn glanced at the window. And right there was a message. The little girl had drawn the peace sign. Above it was a heart with the words "Grace, Mom."

Her father, Chris, and big brother, Jack, also stood up in front of the packed church and read heartfelt letters. Chris looked down at his daughter's casket and asked that she forgive him for not being able to shield her from the gunman.

"I'm so, so sorry," he said, his voice shaking. He paused before thanking her for "bringing so much love, life, and laughter" into his life. "You taught me how to love," he added.

As the small casket was being taken to its final resting place, an emotional rendering of "Amazing Grace" echoed through the church.

Later that morning, twenty-five miles upstate at the Church of the Nativity in Bethlehem, Connecticut, more than a thousand people gathered to mourn the loss of teacher's aide Rachel D'Avino. Family and friends in her hometown took turns recalling fond memories and spoke with conviction of a life that was just beginning to come into full bloom. Working with children was a lifelong goal for Rachel, who had just begun working at the school as a behavioral therapist that fall. There were also wedding bells on the way. Only two days before the shooting, her longtime boyfriend asked her parents for her hand in marriage. He was going to propose to her on Christmas Eve.

Her sister Sarah delivered the eulogy: "That was Rachel, a hard worker, risk taker, a winner. She excelled at everything she did, such as her incredible patience and ability to work with those with special needs, adults and children alike."

. . .

In Trumbull, Connecticut, Mary Sherlach was being remembered as a hero by a standing-room-only crowd at St. Stephen Roman Catholic Church. After the gunfire started, it was Sherlach who, along with Principal Dawn Hochsprung, moved toward the danger while most took cover. Sherlach, the school psychologist at Sandy Hook Elementary School, had planned to retire at year's end to a camp she owned with her husband, Bill, near Owasco Lake, in upstate New York.

Family friend John Simek, who had introduced her to her husband, gave the eulogy, telling loved ones to remember Sherlach for her "love for her neighbors and friends, and always reaching out." She was also remembered for her passion for her students, and her beloved Miami Dolphins. During the funeral, one of the speakers held up a number 13 Dan Marino jersey in her honor.

Later that afternoon, Olivia Rose Engel was remembered by her family as their little angel during an afternoon service at St. Rose of Lima Roman Catholic Church. Inside, a large color photograph of the six-year-old rested on an easel with a cluster of white roses arranged on the floor.

Dan Merton and Julie Pokrinchak, Olivia's godparents, remembered the girl who brought so much joy to the world and loved the color purple. They spoke of her "infectious giggle," which usually came out after telling one of her own jokes, and how she loved sailing with her father, Brian.

In attendance was Officer William Chapman, in full uniform, who had cradled Olivia, providing her with comfort during her final moments, who told her, "I love you. Your mom and dad love you." Tears rolled down his cheeks as he stared sadly at the small casket.

Deacon Don Naiman related the story of Officer Chapman's heroism and tender touch that day, eliciting tears from the crowd. "That officer was the voice of Jesus Christ" to the girl, Deacon Naiman said during his homily. "And I am convinced that he gently passed Olivia to the hands of the Blessed Mother."

As her mourners exited the chapel, they learned that the St. Rose of Lima's Christmas pageant, where Olivia was to play an angel, would be dedicated to her.

It was a sea of purple at the funeral for Dylan Hockley. His eight-year-old brother, Jake, released a dozen purple balloons, Dylan's favorite color, in a somber farewell to his little brother outside the Walnut Hill Community Church in Bethel, Connecticut. His mother, Nicole Hockley, stood at the lectern and gave a touching eulogy, beginning by thanking Anne Marie Murphy.

"Dylan and Mrs. Murphy had a special bond," she said.

Dylan looked at his class picture on the fridge every day and smiled and said, "Here's my class. There's Mrs. Murphy."

Hockley spoke eloquently about channeling the grief and heartache into lasting change.

I once asked him, "Why do you flap?" Because he had under-developed language skills, I was not expecting an answer but he replied, "Because I am a beautiful butterfly." It meant a great deal to us because children with special needs are that much purer and more innocent and the idea of Dylan as a butterfly, now out of the cocoon of his body . . . it comforts me.

It has been said that something as small as a butterfly flapping its wings can cause a hurricane halfway around the world. A small change, a single occurrence in one place, can make large differences elsewhere. It redefines the culture. Dylan is our butterfly. All the children and adults who lost their lives last week are our butterflies. And if one butterfly can cause a hurricane, then twenty-six butterflies can change the world.

SATURDAY:

Josephine Gay, Ana Marquez-Greene, and Emilie Parker

Saturday would be the final day of funerals as the last three students from Lauren Rousseau's class—Josephine Gay, Ana Grace Marquez-Greene, and Emilie Parker—were all laid to rest.

At St. Rose of Lima Roman Catholic Church, Monsignor Weiss was presiding over his eighth funeral for the Sandy Hook community. As he stood over the tiny coffin of Josephine Gay, he couldn't contain his outrage.

As we gather as a community this is the real challenge for us, to think these twenty beautiful children and these six adults, committed to education, were just taken from us. None of it makes sense. You send your child to school in the morning assuming it will be like every other day.

I spent that day with all of you and the other families in the firehouse as names were being called out. We didn't hear little Joey's name. I watched you, Michele. You weren't just lost in yourself that day—you were lost with all of the other mothers, too. I saw you going from parent to parent, sharing with each other that horrible pain and anxiety until that horrible announcement came.

This is a horrible tragedy and it makes no sense to us. We have a lot of issues before us. And if you haven't been angry, get angry. If these twenty children cannot change this world, no one will. They did not die in vain.

Josephine's parents, Michele and Bob, both read eulogies and spoke about some of the "favorite life lessons," they'd learned from their seven-year-old daughter. "She touched so many people. She did not care about prestige or possessions. She calls all of us to be better," her father said.

Later that morning, a carriage drawn by two white horses brought Ana Marquez-Greene to the First Cathedral Church in Bloomfield, Connecticut, where there was a musical celebration in honor of the life she lived. "We've come to celebrate Ana Grace Marquez-Greene," said Archbishop Leroy Bailey. "The only difference now is that she lives in our hearts."

Ana's service was also broadcast live at the Grant Memorial Baptist Church in Winnipeg, Canada, where the family lived before moving to Newtown. Harry Connick Jr. and Javier Colon, the singer who won the first season of *The Voice* TV competition, both serenaded mourners. Ana's father, jazz saxophonist Jimmy Greene, and mother, Nelba, sat in the front row as musicians played the Latin music their daughter loved.

At times, the grief-stricken parents managed to laugh at the memories of Ana singing and dancing as home videos were played of Ana singing "I'm a Little Teapot" and "*Dame la Mano Paloma* (Give Me Your Hand)," her favorite Spanish song.

Ana loved music so much she would dance from room to room with the only sounds coming from somewhere deep within her soul. Reverend Paul Echtenkamp said Ana was born with a musical gift. "Ana had a song. It just came out of her."

Emilie Parker was taken home to Ogden, Utah, the last of the children to be laid to rest. At a Church of Jesus Christ of Latter-day Saints, grieving family and friends of Emilie turned out in droves, most wearing her favorite color—pink. The blond-haired, blue-eyed girl was remembered by family and friends for her wonderful sense of humor.

Her parents emerged from the funeral holding their two other daughters, Madeline and Samantha, both dressed in pink coats. As they drove to take Emilie to her final resting place, in a show of support locals had turned the streets of Ogden pink, with ribbons, bows, and angels attached to trees on the streets leading up to the cemetery.

CHAPTER 16

——◁◇▷——

THE TRIAL OF NANCY LANZA

Ryan Lanza looked out into the rows of pews. Six months had passed since he lost his mother. He had claimed her remains on December 19, and her body was then driven about 170 miles away to Linwood Cemetery & Crematory in Haverhill, Massachusetts, where she was cremated. The next day a small handful of friends and family members quietly gathered at the 1760s-era home on Depot Road in Kingston, New Hampshire, belonging to Nancy's brother James Champion, to mourn their loss.

Now, at her memorial service, Ryan gripped the sides of the lectern, took a deep breath, and began to speak about his loss.

"It dawns on you at a certain point, you realize you will probably bury your parents." He paused to gain his composure. The church was still with quiet reverence as Nancy Lanza's firstborn son spoke lovingly of the attentive mother who never missed a school play, always sitting in the front row of the auditorium to cheer him on. A mother who enriched his life with culture, frequently taking him for tours around the museums of New York City and Washington, D.C., and of course a mother who sat with him at Fenway Park to watch their beloved Boston Red Sox play baseball.

He spoke about a mother who would make the two-hour drive from Sandy Hook, Connecticut, to Hoboken, New Jersey, to sit with him for an hour's lunch before getting in her car and driving two hours back. "She was always there," he said, his eyes tearing up. "Everything I know about baseball . . . everything I know about cooking I know from her."

As he spoke, his father, Peter Lanza, sat in the front row weeping. Dorothy Hanson, Nancy's mother, held a tissue in one hand as she allowed the tears to roll down her cheeks. A group of regulars from My Place Pizza & Restaurant were also in the pews, having met up in the restaurant's parking lot to carpool the nearly two-hundred-mile trip to the First Congregational Church in Kingston, New Hampshire, to pay their final respects to their friend. The 160 mourners sat still in silence staring up at the young man who had lost so much at such a young age.

"She taught me so much . . . And if there is anything I could change, I wouldn't change anything." Ryan spoke in measured tones as he continued, trying to keep the tears bottled up inside. "Even though she's gone, everything's going to be okay," he said, while pausing again to gain his composure. "Her memory will live in my heart and mind."

Outside the church, bagpipes played as a dozen uniformed police officers kept a tight guard over the entrance to ensure that there would be no disturbances and that only friends and family could attend. After the service had concluded, a thirty-car procession, many with the familiar green-and-white stickers that read WE ARE SANDY HOOK. WE CHOOSE LOVE plastered on the bumpers, traveled the short distance to Greenwood Cemetery where her ashes were spread.

"Amazing Grace" played on bagpipes as mourners placed roses at the grave site. Then Erica Schwichtenberg, a friend of Nancy's, played the Beatles song "Here, There and Everywhere" on her violin. It was a song Nancy would often request that she play at open-mike night back at My Place.

After everyone else had finished paying respects, Nancy's mother, Dorothy Hanson, stood alone quietly at her daughter's grave.

Forty miles north of Newtown in Farmington, Connecticut, the remains of Adam Lanza lay in a zipped bag on a gurney in a refrigerated room at the medical examiner's office for thirteen days after the shooting. With most of the media gone, Adam's body was quietly claimed by his father on December 27 and taken to the Linwood Cemetery & Crematory in Haverhill, Massachusetts, where his remains were cremated.

On Friday, December 21, Governor Dan Malloy gathered with other officials on the steps of the town hall as the chiming of twenty-six bells reverberated throughout the state, one time for each victim, commemorating one week since the mass killing. The lives of the twenty-six people murdered by Adam Lanza at Sandy Hook Elementary School in December were eulogized and celebrated after the tragedy.

Of the hundreds of makeshift memorials that had sprung up around Sandy Hook and Newtown, the twenty-six angels, twenty-six flags, twenty-six votive candles, only one could be found that mentioned Nancy Lanza. Scrolled on a yellow piece of paper and hammered to a piece of wood was a message from a friend: "Others now share pain for choices you faced alone. May the blameless among us throw the first stone."

Mark Barden believes that Nancy Lanza bears some of the responsibility for the loss of his seven-year-old son, Daniel. He believes that Nancy could have chosen to go in a different direction instead of feeding her mentally disturbed son's growing firearms obsession by taking him repeatedly to gun ranges and purchasing the high-powered weaponry that she kept in the house. "It all comes down to parenting," said Barden.

Nancy Lanza could have prevented the tragedy if she simply followed the laws on the books in Connecticut requiring adults to keep their firearms safely out of the hands of anyone under the age of twenty-one. The state strictly prohibits anyone under that age to be in possession of a firearm. Adam not only had his own gun safe and access to his own firearms, but police believe his mother encouraged his passion for firearms by frequently taking him to the shooting range.

"Perhaps she could have made some other choices as to how to spend time with her son," said Barden. "How about fishing?"

CHAPTER 17

———◄○►———

THE PERFECT STORM

Liza Long buried her head in her hands. She couldn't stop sobbing. After hearing of the shooting at Sandy Hook, the tears kept coming, streaking down her cheeks. She cried for the victims, their families, their friends, their community, and then finally she cried again—this time for herself.

"When I looked at Nancy Lanza, I saw myself," said Long. "I saw what my son was capable of doing if he didn't get the proper treatment."

That night, in Boise, Idaho, Liza took to her parenting blog, "The Anarchist Soccer Mom," to share the personal day-to-day struggles she has endured in raising her mentally ill son, Michael. She began her post, "I live with a son who is mentally ill. I love my son. But he terrifies me."

She went on to write about a violent episode that had happened shortly before the shooting in Sandy Hook, when her thirteen-year-old suffered an outbreak over an argument about overdue library books. The mother of four tried every technique in her varied repertoire but still couldn't manage to calm her raging son. His anger continued to escalate, culminating with his pulling a knife out and threatening to kill her. Long was forced to call the police.

"That conflict ended with three burly police officers and a paramedic wrestling my son onto a gurney for an expensive ambulance ride to the local emergency room," she wrote. "The mental hospital didn't have any beds that day, and Michael calmed down nicely in the ER, so they sent us home with a prescription for Zyprexa and a follow-up visit with a local pediatric psychiatrist."

Long was out of answers. No one could seem to figure out what was wrong with Michael. After enduring years of watching her son go from doctor to doctor, and being diagnosed with a slew of different afflictions, each one coming with a new medication, and none of them working, it was hard for his struggling mother to feel anything but hopeless. "No one wants to send a thirteen-year-old genius who loves Harry Potter, and his snuggle-animal collection to jail. But our society, with its stigma on mental illness and its broken health care system, does not provide us with other options," she wrote.

She ended with a plea: "It's time for a meaningful, nationwide conversation about mental health. That's the only way our nation can ever truly heal."

Liza titled the piece "I Am Adam Lanza's Mother."

The post went viral. Since first posted on December 15, it has been viewed more than six million times, sparking a nationwide conversation that opened up the debate on the role of mental health in the shooting at Sandy Hook and of the condition of the mental health system in the United States. While most of the feedback on her article was positive, Long also came under attack. Many were outraged by the post, believing that Long's post attempted to justify the mass killings and was insulting to the memory of the victims. Others scoured her other online writings, attacking her parenting and questioning her decision to go public with her child's mental illness.

"I have been under attack since I came out and opened up about my struggles with my son's mental illness, but I think it's a fight worth making," said Long. "I just kept thinking, if I don't stand up now, then when?"

Now Long finds herself front and center in the debate on mental health in this country. Suddenly in demand by the national media, she has trouble keeping up with all the requests for her to speak at different mental health groups. She is also writing a book on autism and the inadequate state of mental health care in America.

"I used to be in the shadows myself. What happened in Sandy Hook has been a transformative process for me. I knew I had to act. If a tragedy of this magnitude doesn't open up the conversation, then I'm afraid nothing ever will," said Long.

Her son Michael is in many ways brilliant. He has an encyclopedic mind when it comes to Greek mythology. He is caring and thoughtful of other people. If his mother or a friend needs help, he is quick to volunteer. In many ways he shows maturity well beyond his thirteen years. However, when his mental illness takes over, he can feel himself morphing into a person he barely recognizes. His mind goes blank and the violent impulses take over.

"I feel backed into a corner and I have to attack or get away.

I can't think about anything else," Michael said. "It's kind of like a werewolf. When a werewolf turns into a werewolf, it doesn't know who he is, it doesn't know where he is, it just wants to hurt and fight people. You can't control yourself when you're like that, and no one else can."

The list of diagnoses reads like a catalog: sensory integration disorder, oppositional defiant disorder, intermittent explosive disorder, ADHD, anxiety, depression, autistic spectrum disorder, juvenile bipolar disorder, post-traumatic stress syndrome, and dysgraphia.

The list of medications prescribed during his short thirteen-year life are equally troubling: Abilify, risperdone, clonidine, trazodone, Concerta, Ritalin, Daytrana patch, Celexa, guanfacine, Zyprexa, and currently Intuniv, Wellbutrin, lithium, and Trileptal. He sees a psychiatrist, an occupational therapist, a psychologist, has psychosocial rehabilitation once a week, and has a Department of Health and Welfare caseworker.

"For mothers of special needs children, the quest to find proper treatment can become all consuming," Long said. She has good health insurance, but because of her son's therapeutic care, medications, and babysitting costs, she typically spends one-third of her paycheck on Michael's needs.

Still, Long is counting her blessings, knowing that despite the problems she has with her son, there are others who have it much worse. "I have it easy compared to some other parents I know whose kids are suffering from mental illness. My son isn't burning things or killing animals."

· · ·

Nancy Lanza spent the years when her son Adam was between nine and seventeen consumed by the search to help cure his affliction. As a young child Adam was in a constant state of struggle with the world around him. At the age of five, Adam Lanza was diagnosed with Asperger's syndrome, and shortly afterward, a second condition, sensory processing disorder.

As Adam got older, he struggled to fit in and couldn't relate to his peers, and as his condition worsened, he made the decision to spend less time in the outside world and instead sought comfort in the delusional fantasy world of violence and death he had created in his own mind. By the time Adam was nineteen, he had withdrawn almost completely and become a virtual shut-in, spending hours playing the first-person shooter game *Call of Duty*. In the months that preceded the shooting, Adam began to isolate himself in his bedroom, surrounded all day and all night by violent images.

Nancy Lanza had the financial resources to see any doctor in the state, but by 2008 she told a friend that finding adequate treatment for her son had become "a lost cause."

"He's so bright, but no one is willing to give him the time and attention he deserves," she frequently told a family member.

Marianne Kristiansson, a professor of forensic psychiatry at Karolinska Institute in Stockholm, Sweden, published a recent study looking at the characteristics of violent offenders who also had autism. Kristiansson pointed out that the vast majority of those with autism are law-abiding citizens who will never commit any crimes but, out of the small sample of mass killers she looked at, a higher representation of autism was found to be prevalent. Based on her knowledge of what is publicly known about Adam Lanza, she believes it was his inability to express his frustrations that ultimately led to the massacre.

"The behavior of Adam Lanza was quite typical of a subject with autism," said Kristiansson. "This behavior is impossible to understand because it's so horrible. The motive is different from what you would normally see in a criminal. You want to communicate on a very global level that people have treated you in a very bad way and you want revenge.

"Many of the offenders we have looked at wanted to communicate to other authorities that they are very offended and very frustrated, but due to their autistic traits, they didn't have the ability to communicate that verbally, so instead they acted out in these bizarre and odd ways."

After studying Peter Mangs, a forty-year-old with a diagnosis of Asperger's who was charged with shooting more than a dozen people from 2009 to 2010, Kristiansson found that it was his inability to communicate his dissatisfaction with society that ultimately drove him to kill. "I'm quite sure that Adam Lanza was offended by the school, his community, his mother, and others but he wasn't able to verbalize this dissatisfaction," said Kristiansson. "Part of autistic traits is that people like Adam can't think about how other people might feel, they can only think from their own perspective, so it all became about him making a statement saying that he was extremely offended by the school and wanted revenge."

Still, most in the medical community believe there is no link between autism and acts of violence and that the accusations further damage an already stigmatized and targeted group of people. Most autism groups dispute the science that links autism to violence. Most believe the studies are flawed and cite studies of their own that show there is no link.

"There is absolutely no evidence or any reliable research that suggests a linkage between autism and planned violence," the Autism Society said in a statement. "To imply or suggest that some linkage exists is wrong and is harmful to more than 1.5 million law-abiding, nonviolent, and wonderful individuals who live with autism each day."

Many children with autism already face enough societal challenges without being linked to mass shootings, according to Peter Bell of Autism Speaks. "Autism did not commit this horrible act. A man did," said Bell, executive vice president for programs and services for the advocacy and research group. "We are an evidence-based organization and when you look at the scientific literature there really is no connection between autism and acts of violence," explained Bell, who is also the father of a son with autism "In fact, we find evidence that supports the fact that they are usually the victims.

"We were saddened to see the media jump on the idea that this was Asperger's. There were a number of autistic victims involved in this tragedy and because of that we've been impacted emotionally."

Bell believes that there is also a misperception that those with autism don't feel empathy. "They are highly empathic and the research supports that," says Bell.

Nicole Hockley, whose autistic son Dylan was one of the victims in the shooting, bristles at any suggestion that links her son's condition with violence. "It's highly offensive and damaging to link autism and violence and it isn't backed up by science," Hockley said.

"We are talking about some of the most caring, compassionate people you would ever meet. He was very empathic. He loved to laugh and be tickled. Dylan was just so pure and full of love."

Still, the medical community remains divided.

"The mental health community is extremely sensitive about linking violence with autism; many refuse to make the link but the facts tell a different story," said Dr. Edward Shorter, a professor of the history of medicine and psychiatry in the Faculty of Medicine of the University of Toronto who has published numerous books on the subject. "Autistic children often have trouble understanding the normal rules of society. They don't understand the proper way to behave in social settings and can tend to seek isolation," Dr. Shorter said. "This can lead to violent behavior."

Liza Long says she draws on her own personal experience and that "countless" emails of support from other struggling parents of autistic kids are proof that a problem exists. "The violent behavior is the elephant in the room with the autism community. How do we begin to fix it if we can't even acknowledge it?

"To say that the potential of violence isn't a factor with autistic kids just isn't true. We are talking about a community of very unique people who see the world in a different way from the rest of us and have different triggers."

In many ways Liza Long's obstacles with her son have mirrored Nancy Lanza's plight with Adam. For Michael, it appeared that one big behavioral turning point came when trying to make the transition from elementary school to middle school, where he couldn't adjust to changing classes, becoming overwhelmed by the sounds and lights. Adam had similar struggles with the transition.

"For someone like my son, from a sensory integration standpoint, there couldn't be a worse place for him. The large fluorescent lights are always on. It was never quiet. It could literally put him right in a state of psychosis," Long said.

Michael is also prone to becoming easily fixated, but fortunately for Long her son obsesses over stuffed animals and Greek mythology, not violent video games and firearms. Because of her own experience, Liza Long shudders when she sees the news reports of only twenty-six victims, believing that Adam Lanza was a victim of his mental illness and of a society that hasn't given the proper attention and tools to appropriately deal with it.

"It is obvious just by looking at pictures of Adam that he wasn't getting the proper treatment," Long added. "Adam was absolutely responsible for his actions, but that doesn't mean he wasn't a victim.

"Adam Lanza was a mentally ill man who did an evil act, then committed suicide. Adam is a victim of not having the access to the resources to get him the proper treatment. He's a victim of his parents' crumbling marriage, which is hell on earth for special needs children.

"Adam Lanza is the twenty-eighth victim."

In the days immediately following the tragedy in Sandy Hook, news reporters from around the country began scouring the town for any morsel of information they could find from former friends or classmates who knew Adam Lanza. "I knew of him, but I didn't know him," was the common refrain from young men who were about Adam's age.

When seemingly everyone was connected through social media outlets such as Facebook and Twitter, it seemed impossible that anyone could hide so completely, especially after having lived in the same small town of 27,000. Adam Lanza managed to become the closest thing to anonymous anyone could find in a tight-knit community such as Newtown. The Lanza home rarely had visitors. Within Nancy's small pocket of friends, only a few had been inside her house over the past two years. Adam would go several weeks at a time without leaving the house or talking to another human being other than his mother. Few noticed. Those who did chalked it up to his "strangeness."

When Nicole Hockley, whose son Dylan died in the Sandy Hook shooting, spoke at a community safety meeting, she told the audience that even before the shooting occurred, the Lanza home was the only one that wasn't completely part of the community— "a black spot in the neighborhood."

"No one spoke about them. I've never heard a neighbor speak of them. Perhaps if there was more engagement within a community with neighbors looking out for each other, supporting each other, then maybe they would have gotten help in a different sort of way. But to know everyone on your street except for one house, and that happens to be a house with people that—or a person who does this—that's kind of hard to swallow. So there is some regret there."

Of the few people aware that Nancy Lanza's son was troubled, most of them assumed that she was dealing with it. Outwardly,

Nancy rarely talked about or displayed the kind of internal stress she was experiencing with her son.

"Nancy always put on a happy face. She wasn't the kind of person who felt comfortable talking about her personal problems or complaining," said one relative. "We knew she was having problems with Adam not wanting to leave the house, but no one knew to what extent."

John Cacioppo, a social psychologist at the University of Chicago in Illinois, has researched the effects of isolation on the human mind and believes severe cases can cause several potentially unhealthy changes in perception that can ultimately lead to violence. "Isolation isn't at all what people thought it was, and it's a lot more important than people thought it was," Cacioppo says. "No matter what social species you're talking about, all the way down to fruit flies, if you isolate them they die earlier. It lowers your impulse control and essentially triggers a self-preservation mind-set. A lonely person's brain is always on the lookout for social threats."

If a social person sees someone else in trouble, they are more likely to help because they feel empathy, but if a lonely person sees someone else in trouble it triggers a self-preservation instinct because they don't have anyone to take care of them, according to Cacioppo. He noted that lonely people show heightened focus on negative thoughts and perceptions. They also tend to find greater fault with themselves and those around them; they expect others to be less friendly, less kind. They're bracing against "social threats," but those expectations have a way of fulfilling themselves, Cacioppo says. In the negative-feedback loop of chronic loneliness, self-protection turns out to be self-defeat.

The effect can be even worse for isolated people who seek comfort on the Internet. People who use the Internet to generate or enhance in-person relationships can benefit, while those who use online connections as a substitute for face-to-face ones become lonelier and more depressed. "Isolated people can become fixated on their immediate environment. If that environment is guns and violence, it has the potential to lead to problems," Cacioppo said.

For up to fourteen hours a day, Adam sat alone in his windowless basement playing violent video games in the months leading up to the savage shooting. Sometimes he dressed from head to toe in a military uniform like the character in the game as he shot at paper targets with a pellet gun.

"He is like a zombie in front of the screen," Nancy Lanza complained just two weeks before she was found murdered in her bed.

Many wanted to blame the video games. The tragedy at Sandy Hook wasn't the first time the graphic gore-filled war games had been linked to a mass shooting. Norwegian murderer Anders Behring Breivik credited the game *Call of Duty* with having helped him in his preparations before his killing spree. *World of Warcraft*, a violent fantasy game, was reportedly one of the video games that James Holmes, the suspect in the Aurora movie theater shooting, frequently played. Eric Harris and Dylan Klebold went on their shooting rampage at Columbine High School after their parents took away their video game privileges.

Psychologists have voiced concerns that spending prolonged amounts of time surrounded by violent images can blur the line between fiction and reality, possibly leading to devastating consequences. "When we hand a child a controller and put them in the position of controlling a gun and repeatedly making it shoot human beings, we are desensitizing them to real world violence and making them less empathetic to suffering," explained Joanne Cantor, an expert on the psychological effects of media and a professor emerita at the University of Madison, Wisconsin.

Not surprisingly, younger children are most at risk of being influenced by America's addiction to violence. Imagery we see when we're younger than thirteen leaves a particularly lasting imprint, and children under five are almost completely unable to differentiate fiction from reality, according to Cantor.

Today's sheer amount of blood and gore in the gaming industry is unprecedented in modern history, experts say. Still, the causes of violence are complex and cannot be simplified by concluding that exposure to violent images alone is the driving reason behind the recent spate of mass shootings.

"There is no evidence that a single violent crime has come from a video game," said Cheryl K. Olson, a public health researcher and coauthor of *Grand Theft Childhood: The Surprising Truth About Violent Video Games and What Parents Can Do.* "If you look at someone like Adam Lanza, who isolated himself for hours at a time in front of these games, it is clear that it can create a violent situation, but that's true if you sit in front of anything for too long in isolation."

Olson's research showed that an average child in seventh and eighth grade plays at least one violent video game on a regular basis; meanwhile, as the trend of violent video games increases, violent crimes as a whole have decreased. It appears that for normal healthy kids, violent video games have no correlation with real-world violence. On the whole, these well-balanced children have a surprisingly good understanding of the difference between fantasy and reality, according to Olson.

"In a video game they know it is violence and can act out that violence in a fantasy world, but there is no evidence that video games cause a desensitization to real-world violence," she explained. "The real abnormal part was how he cut himself off from other people, not that he played violent video games."

A pattern has emerged in the recent mass killings in Connecticut, Colorado, Norway, and elsewhere, when young men whose social isolation borders on autism become prey to psychotic ideation and, under its influence, commit acts of horrible violence.

"We have created a recipe for a time bomb and Adam Lanza is right in the middle of that pot," says Dr. Edward Shorter. "Autism and psychosis are two separate illnesses, but they can come together in today's ultraviolent culture in a horrible way."

This represents a large cultural shift that began in the 1960s, reflecting the increasing power of violent images that pervade everyday life on the minds of disturbed young men. While overall violent crimes are trending downward, mass shootings are becoming more common. Six of the twelve deadliest shootings to take place in American history have happened in the last six years.

"Young men suffering from delusions a hundred years ago were often more fixated on a perceived slight from a boss at work or their mother," says Shorter. "Today young men with delusional thinking are filled with violent ideas from culture and video games and have the ability to surround themselves with guns and death in a way that is unprecedented in all of history.

"The more someone with Adam's symptoms immerses himself

in the world of these superviolent video games, the more they lose context with reality and are prone to act in these violent ways."

During bouts of isolation, paranoia can begin to set in and those afflicted with autism can lose all sense of reality. "In cases where an adolescent acquires a particular set of delusions they can convince themselves that they can help society by fighting against the oppressor," said Shorter, who claims that his studies of case records dating back over the past one hundred years shows that the amount of violence and delusional thinking has increased significantly. "In many cases we are talking about people who also believe the world is conspiring to oppress them. It is very popular in right-wing circles among gun lovers who fear the government is conspiring to take their firearms away.

"It's simple. If someone loses all sense of reality, and isolates themselves in an environment of violence, it's a very short step to acting it out," Shorter added. "You throw in access to weapons that can fire off one hundred and fifty shots in five minutes and look out. This gives them the means of acting on their delusions, and acting out those delusions can be a natural progression."

Until the morning of December 14, Newtown was synonymous with Fairfield Hills State Hospital, a psychiatric hospital located near the center of town. The facility was built in 1931 over 186 rolling green acres situated at the highest point in town. Part of its purpose was to help alleviate the overcrowding at other neighboring mental hospitals. The sixteen buildings, all connected by underground tunnels, were home to more than four thousand patients when filled to capacity. "Better watch yourself or you're gonna be sent to Newtown" had become a popular threat in the neighboring areas to anyone exhibiting behavior that strayed too far from the norm.

Beginning in 1955 with the widespread introduction of Thorazine, the first effective antipsychotic medication, America began one of the largest social experiments in history, the deinstitutionalizing of the mentally ill. By the 1960s and 1970s, Fairfield Hills steadily began to lose patients as part of the initiative to shut down large mental health facilities. It wasn't just happening in Newtown. It signified a dramatic shift going on nationwide to replace long-stay psychiatric hospitals with less isolated community mental health services.

The results were drastic. In 1955 there were 558,239 severely mentally ill patients in the nation's public psychiatric hospitals. By 1994, despite the population boom, that number had been reduced to 71,619.

On December 8, 1995, Fairfield Hills was closed by the state of Connecticut. The entrances to the underground tunnels that had attracted thrill seekers were sealed. Many rooms of the abandoned buildings are still filled with office equipment, wheelchairs, patient files, and gurneys as if suspended in time. In 2001, the town bought the property from the state and plans are now in place to bulldoze the remaining buildings. A current proposal on the table would replace them with a retail strip and restaurants.

As the mental institutions continued to close, in many states the money slowly began to dry up. In recent years when state budgets across the country needed trimming, mental health services were often among the first to go. In the past three years, $4.35 billion has been cut from state budgets across the country, according to a report by the National Association of State Mental Health Program Directors Research Institute. As states slash funding for treatment, private care is getting increasingly more difficult to find. Many private care facilities don't take insurance.

While today there is little debate in the mental health community over the merit of shuttering the large institutions, many of which were fraught with allegations of patient abuse and neglect, experts believe that the community mental health services that were supposed to serve in their place have in many ways failed and that a shortage of quality medical care is pervasive in the mental health community.

"Finding a good doctor is a tremendous problem," said Dr. Michael Friedman, an adjunct associate professor at the Columbia University Schools of Social Work. "In this country we have a shortage of competent professionals to treat people with mental issues. It is very rare that people seeking professional help receive anything above minimally adequate service."

Part of the problem lies in the fact that most general physicians aren't properly trained to identify and understand mental health problems. "Doctors just aren't equipped to deal well with the kind of complaints coming from parents who have children in the autism spectrum," Friedman said.

Another problem is the tendency that still exists among some within the medical community to dismiss mental illness. Rates of psychosis are higher in autistics and, in many cases, psychotic symptoms may go undiagnosed and untreated because they're written off as just part of the autism spectrum.

"A doctor hears from a mother that her child is nonsocial and oftentimes there is no obvious prescription, so the parent is told the child will grow out of it. That doesn't happen. These are conditions and need to be taken seriously for everyone's sake," Dr. Shorter said.

In most ways, the mental health system in America has never been better, according to Friedman, but the science of understanding the human brain is still in its infancy and asking doctors to appropriately identify mental illness is a challenging task. "It is very difficult for even good clinicians to make good mental health diagnoses. The best experts in the world have trouble in this area."

While closing the mental institutions was a great idea in theory, the problem is that they've been replaced with jails, not the community outreach programs that were originally intended. "When the government came up with the idea to deinstitutionalize, the plan was to get these people out of the big institutions and into community outreach programs. But we don't have adequate community outreach programs and instead we have jails," said Liza Long. "We closed these institutions without an adequate community care system in place and now it is blowing up in our faces."

In many states, insurance companies still don't include treatment for autism in their coverage. "Getting access to care is still difficult. The fact that many insurance companies still exclude autism treatments is something that we've been working on changing," said Peter Bell of Autism Speaks.

Finding solutions, like seemingly all aspects of mental health, is complicated. Dr. Sreedhar Potarazu, a medical expert and founder and CEO of VitalSpring Technologies Inc., believes that one of the contributing problems is the large number of young adult men who are suffering from depression and have no place to go. "If you were to survey the freshman class of many Ivy League schools you would find that forty percent are on some kind of medication for anxiety or depression," said Potarazu. "There are so many young adults in need of care and very limited resources exist to help them."

Potarazu worries that the medical community still hasn't fully recognized the gravity of the mental health issue. "Depression or anxiety is no different from diabetes in many respects. It is a chemical imbalance in the brain and needs to be treated but there is often a failure to recognize that in the medical community," he said. "We don't do enough in terms of identifying and treating those in need. I believe we need to do more early screening in terms of understanding those who are at risk. We screen for a whole range of things, why not for mental illness?"

Potarazu believes that if mental illness had been spotted earlier, then perhaps some of these shootings could have been stopped. "If you look at these mass shooters, this isn't their first incident. They all have histories. The warning signs were all right there for anyone to look at and see."

There is a growing movement within the mental health community for pediatric primary care providers to attend to the developmental, behavioral, and mental health needs of children and adolescents in their practices. But that, too, would present challenges. "The integration is a necessary step but it won't be an easy one," said Dr. Friedman. "The science of mental health is very complicated."

The expansion of Medicaid, under the 2010 health care reform law, should expand access to mental health services to the previously uninsured. The law will require all health insurers to cover mental health services on a basis similar to other kinds of health care, and health insurance plans sold in the new state exchanges will be required to include mental health coverage.

"That's a good place to start, but it won't make any difference if the care people are receiving continues to be inadequate," said Friedman. He wonders if perhaps people shouldn't look to the mental health community at all to stop these kinds of shootings. "I don't believe that any change or advances in the way of mental health in this country are going to have a significant impact on mass murders. These mass shootings are so rare, what do you change?"

Moving forward, Liza Long would like to see a mental health crisis team that parents can call instead of 911, and mental health centers where parents can walk in and their children can get treatment. "As parents we have a responsibility to fight for better treatments for our kids."

But for Long, the first step comes back to acknowledging the problem. "I'm going to keep fighting until there is a change to our mental health system," she said. "I may have written 'I Am Adam Lanza's Mother,' but I'm determined that I'm not going to be Nancy Lanza."

· · ·

On June 3, President Obama delivered remarks at the National Conference on Mental Health to challenge the country to act on what he believes to be a mental health crisis. "The main goal of this conference is not to start a conversation," he said in opening remarks at the White House. "Instead, it's about elevating that conversation to a national level and bringing mental illness out of the shadows."

He read off the statistics: one in five adults experience a mental illness and forty-five million Americans suffer from depression or anxiety, schizophrenia or PTSD. "We've got to get rid of that embarrassment; we've got to get rid of that stigma. Too many Americans who struggle with mental health illnesses are still suffering in silence rather than seeking help, and we need to see to it that men and women who would never hesitate to go see a doctor if they had a broken arm or came down with the flu, that they have that same attitude when it comes to their mental health.

"We see it in parents who would do anything for their kids, but who often fight their mental health battle alone—afraid that reaching out would somehow reflect badly on them.

"We see it in the tragedies that we have the power to prevent."

CHAPTER 18

———◄◦►———

GLORY KILLER

It wasn't mental illness that caused the horrors of December 14 but the work of a depraved psychopath, according to investigators. Adam Lanza knew exactly what he was doing as he carefully crafted his terror spree to maximize bloodshed and shock the world, said a law enforcement source familiar with the killer's various journals and writings found inside the Lanza home at 36 Yogananda Street.

"It wasn't mental illness that drove him to walk into Sandy Hook Elementary that day," the official explained. "This was a young man who knew exactly what he was doing."

The seven handwritten journals and numerous drawings and charts show a depraved indifference to human life that exhibited itself through psychopathic behavior. "Human life was nothing to him. Shooting up the kids wasn't a cry for help. He didn't break from reality. Killing these kids was fun for him. We are talking about a cold-blooded killer," the official said.

If his initial attack proves to be Newtown High School, that could indicate a broader need to communicate his grievances and express his emotions that he felt he was wronged.

"Adam was angry. Newtown High School was his only real connection to the outside world and suddenly it was taken away from him and it must have seemed to him quite unfair," said Richard Novia, Adam's Tech Club advisor and former head of security at the school. "I believe he blamed the school and this terrible shooting was his sick way of telling the world."

While the condition of "psychopathy" is not recognized by most mainstream medical journals, it is a common diagnostic tool used by law enforcement and criminal profilers to analyze behavior. In her work as a criminal profiler for the FBI, Mary Ellen O'Toole came face-to-face with countless murderers and serial killers who she believes fall under the label of psychopath. And based on what is known of Adam's life and her knowledge of the crime scene, O'Toole believes that Adam Lanza displayed clear psychopathic traits.

"I would not classify this kind of behavior as that of someone who is mentally ill. Blaming this on mental illness conveys that Adam was out of touch with reality. There is no doubt Adam had serious issues, but we are talking about a crime that was extremely callous and deliberate, with all of the traits of a psychopath," O'Toole said. "Adam made a conscious decision to go shoot those children in Sandy Hook Elementary. He knew it was wrong and the thought of the violence thrilled him."

A psychopath is defined by the primary characteristic of an inability to show empathy for others. The sheer horror of the killing,

first with his mother then followed by the cold-blooded execution of six teachers and twenty children, was a textbook example
of psychopathic behavior, according to O'Toole. "He was very self-
focused. Over the course of time he trained his mind to view hu-
mans more as objects," she said.

For most people, the idea that someone may enjoy violence for
the sake of violence is a tough one to swallow, which is why it's
more comfortable for people to ascribe such incomprehensible acts
to mental illness, O'Toole explained. "People have the tendency to
look at such a horrific crime and say, 'Whoever did this must be
crazy,' but when we look at the planning involved it tells a different
story. How secretive was Adam? How strategic? Did it make sense
or was it sloppy? Was the crime scene cold-blooded and predatory?
Once you begin pulling out behaviors a pattern begins to emerge of
good cognitive strategic skills that are maintained over an extended
period of time."

All violence is not equal, according to O'Toole, who believes
the crime scene at Sandy Hook was instrumental violence, the preferred violence of a psychopathic individual. "It is cold-blooded violence. In these cases victims tend to be strangers. It is purposeful
and well-planned out. It is goal-directed. That is what we have at
Sandy Hook.

"You have children crying, screaming, maybe getting sick, and
his shooting seems to get even more focused as opposed to all over
the place. He was thinking clearly before the crime, during the
crime, and after the crime. Adam's crime was not sloppy. It was
not disorganized. It was well thought out and well-planned. And he
planned this for a long time. You just can't go in and out of reality

for that amount of time. You really have to be analytical to do what he did," said O'Toole.

In choosing Sandy Hook Elementary School as his target, Adam would be able to accomplish two goals: increasing his death count and exerting his control with very little resistance, O'Toole argues. "Control is a big issue for killers in mission-oriented cases. Adam was on almost a military-like mission to kill as many people as possible. He used the element of surprise. He was overly armed. There was no time to talk, just to kill as many people as possible.

"It gives them a sense of omniscience and God-like power they can take life away," continued O'Toole. "He can make the world stop. Killing one or two people doesn't get you the attention anymore. He chose something as terrible and awful as possible to ensure he would get maximum publicity."

Under this scenario Adam would have chosen his mother as his first victim for a more practical reason. "He didn't want her to interfere with his mission," O'Toole said. "If she saw him packing his car with guns she could have called the police. For Adam, carrying out his mission was all consuming."

Investigators also believe Adam's obsession with mass killers wasn't due to mental illness or autistic tendencies to become fixated, but instead a way for him to learn new killing tactics in hopes of topping them all to achieve a level of fame and glory. When Adam frequented Wikipedia, using the screen name "Kaynbred" to meticulously correct entries about mass killers, he was really trying to learn from their experiences, law enforcement believes. The seven-by four-foot-long chart discovered in Adam's room that listed the names, number of kills, and weapons used by the most brutal mass

killers throughout history was likely a scorecard that he was hoping
to top with his name.

"You aren't going to get that level of fame if you just kill a few
people. Killers like Adam liked to watch what gets attention on the
news and the Internet and they try to top it. They think they can
do it better than the guy in Norway and better than Eric and Dylan
in Columbine," said an official with knowledge of the investigation.

The term "psychopathy" is a controversial one within the medical community. Many believe the word oversimplifies other mental issues and has been co-opted by Hollywood in its portrayal of
characters like Patrick Bateman in *American Psycho*. Dr. Marianne
Kristiansson, the Swedish expert in criminal behavior, believes
examples of violent psychopathy are extremely rare and that this
explanation does not fit the characteristics of the crime at Sandy
Hook Elementary.

"Adam was far from being a psychopath. We have to look at the
mechanism that drives the behavior of a psychopath and we don't
see that here," said Kristiansson, who believes mental illness was the
driving force behind this mass killing. "A psychopath would never
commit such a crime," says Kristiansson. "A psychopath tends to
commit crimes that he receives some benefit from, and they rarely
commit suicide."

If Adam was a psychopath, it wouldn't be as rare as most people
would imagine. It is estimated that psychopaths make up 1 percent
of the general population and as much as 25 percent of the male offenders in federal correctional settings. The science of psychopathy
is still in its infancy, but increasingly researchers are concluding that
there may be a physical component. According to a study in *JAMA*

Psychiatry, psychopaths are unable to relate to others because their brains aren't wired to do so. The researchers used brain-imaging technology to track subjects' responses to a scenario where people were being purposely hurt. They found that psychopaths had less activation in certain parts of their brain and high activation in other parts, compared with people who were not psychopaths.

Jean Decety, a professor in psychology and psychiatry who specializes in developmental neuroscience, affective neuroscience, and social neuroscience, says that his research indicates that psychopaths lack the basic neurophysiological hardwiring that enables them to feel empathy for others. Decety led a study involving eighty prisoners between the ages of eighteen and fifty at a correctional facility. The criminals were tested for levels of psychopathy using standard measures, then studied with functional MRI technology to determine their responses to a series of scenarios depicting people being intentionally hurt and short videos of facial expressions showing pain.

The study showed that psychopaths processed empathy, especially in response to the perception of other people in distress, differently than other people.

Regardless of the cause, there is a feeling among some experts that while violent crime as a whole has been going down, these random mass shootings may be a rising trend. "Over the past twenty-five years we have seen an increase in these kind of gratuitous glory killings, where the shooter wants to kill as many strangers as possible. When you start looking at the motivations, that is a phenomenon we have not seen before and the question is if this is not decreasing will it increase in the years to come?" said O'Toole.

CHAPTER 19

———◄◊►———

THE NEWTOWN EFFECT

On the morning of February 27, Neil Heslin sat down at the end of a long table, a box of tissues within arm's reach, and began to give his testimony to the Senate Judiciary Hearing in an eleventh-hour bid to win congressional support for an assault weapons ban. His hands gripped a large portrait of his son, Jesse, a first-grader who was murdered at Sandy Hook Elementary. The grieving father began by telling lawmakers the story of the day he lost his "best friend," part of his emotional plea for lawmakers to act and pass legislation that would ban sales of the types of firearms that had ended the life of his son just ten weeks earlier.

"My name is Neil Heslin. Jesse Lewis was my son. He was a boy who loved life and lived it to the fullest. He was my best friend. On December 14, he lost his life at Sandy Hook Elementary because of a gun that nobody needs and nobody should have a right to have. I'm here to tell his story. I know what I am doing here today won't bring my son back, but I hope that maybe if you listen to what I say today and you do something about it—maybe nobody else will have to experience what I have experienced."

As he continued, a group of Newtown families and residents sitting behind him wiped away tears. Some broke out into sobs.

"Some guns just don't have any place in the hands of civilians. The assault weapons we're talking about today, their sole purpose is to put a lot of lead out in a battlefield quickly. That's what they do. That's what they did at Sandy Hook Elementary. That wasn't a killing; it was a massacre. Those guns and those clips let Adam Lanza massacre those kids. And my son was one of them."

Heslin asked the crowd made up of legislators and law enforcement professionals if anyone could explain to him the need for military-style weapons in the home.

"Second Amendment shall not be infringed!" a gun-rights supporter shouted out, breaking the stillness in the room. "Shall not infringe on our rights."

The man was quickly silenced and escorted out of the building, but his message had been heard by everyone. The battle over gun control would be one fought passionately on both sides of the political spectrum.

Only two and a half months had passed since twenty children and six educators were shot at Sandy Hook Elementary, but in that short amount of time, many of the families had unified around a single issue: reforming the nation's gun laws.

Those grieving over their lost loved ones found themselves with a unique moral authority, admired by a nation that both shared in their grief and was captivated by their tragic stories. In their search to harness the heartache in a way they hoped might prevent future tragedies, they formed Sandy Hook Promise. It began as a small grassroots effort to push for changes in current gun laws as well as reforms in the mental health system and quickly morphed into an organization with a national stage.

The group of fifteen families joined local activists and a handful of key figures in the Democratic Party who all had the mutual goal of reforming gun laws. It was aligned with democratic strategist Ricki Seidman, who had formerly served as Vice President Joe Biden's communications director during the 2008 general election. Seidman went to work helping the families strategize. All media requests were funneled through Lara Bergthold, a veteran Democratic operative now with Griffin Schein, a public relations firm based out of Los Angeles.

With help from the outside groups, the families became a force to be reckoned with on Capitol Hill. The grieving family members turned into powerful lobbyists. They were granted unprecedented access to lawmakers in their push for "common sense" gun reforms.

Tim Makris, a father of a fourth-grader who survived the rampage, quit his product development job to become the group's executive director. "It is time for a national conversation in our community and in Congress about responsibility and accountability. We know there are millions of people in this nation who agree with us," said Makris at a January press conference to announce their goals.

By late January newscasters and politicians had coined the term "the Newtown Effect" to describe the families' unique ability to sway public opinion. The national conversation they sought over assault weapons had gained momentum, dominating the front pages of newspapers nationwide and the twenty-four-hour cable news cycle. Many believed an assault weapons ban was all but inevitable.

Still, if the families were to achieve their legislative victory, they would have to defeat one of the most powerful interest groups in the country: the National Rifle Association and its more than four and a half million members. The NRA also had an ally in Mark Mattioli, whose six-year-old son, James, was killed inside Sandy Hook Elementary. The other Newtown families were misdirecting their energies by focusing primarily on firearms, according to Mattioli, who believed the real solution could be found in mental health legislation.

He made his case to state legislators at an emotional hearing on gun control in January in Hartford, Connecticut. "I don't care if you named [the gun law] 'James's law,' I don't want it," Mattioli said. "I think there's much more promise for a solution in identifying, researching, and creating solutions along the lines of mental health."

Other Second Amendment advocates argued that proposed laws to ban assault weapons, limiting the number of bullets allowed per clip, or increasing background checks would do little or nothing to reduce violence. Professor James Jacobs, a criminologist at New York University, believes that none of the proposed legislation would have prevented the shooting at Newtown or have any real impact on the rate of violent crimes.

"The laws would have virtually no effect. They would do nothing except maybe score points with some voters," says Jacobs, author of *Can Gun Control Work?*

The laws already on the books in Connecticut made Adam Lanza's possession of any guns illegal. He was only twenty years old at the time of the killing, and Connecticut law prohibits anyone under the age of twenty-one from owning a gun. Adam broke another law when he carried his two semiautomatic handguns and a semiautomatic rifle onto school property, which is a felony, unless given prior permission by the school. Other proposals to screen gun owners for mental health issues would not have applied, since the guns Adam used were purchased by his mother, Nancy.

Jacobs is also quick to point out that despite the increase in weapons, violent crime rates have been trending downward for decades. According to the FBI, violent crime has been steadily declining. In 2011, an estimated 1,203,564 violent crimes occurred nationwide, a decrease of 3.8 percent from the 2010 estimate. The 2011 estimated violent crime total was 15.4 percent below the 2007 level and 15.5 percent below the 2002 level.

"The idea that we are in the midst of an epidemic of violence is pure fantasy," says Jacobs. "If anything, we are experiencing an epidemic of nonviolence."

Banning assault guns would merely be "feel good" legislation, according to Jacobs, who says the main difference between weapons that fall under the label "assault" and those that don't is purely cosmetic. "Assault weapons do the same thing as handguns. They shoot the same bullets. The only difference is that they look scary," said Jacobs.

Less than two months later, the bill to ban assault weapons was defeated by a 40–60 vote. A separate amendment introduced by Senator Richard Blumenthal to limit the size of magazines to ten rounds also failed with a vote of 46–54. It was a blow to President Obama's agenda and a larger blow to the Newtown families. As the votes were read, many of them watched from the Senate gallery and broke out in tears.

On the six-month anniversary of the shooting, two hundred people gathered outside the Edmond Town Hall to remember the victims of Sandy Hook Elementary School with twenty-six seconds of silence—one for each slain student and teacher.

"Although it has been six months, we have not forgotten and we will never forget the ones who have died," Carlee Soto declared at 9:37 A.M. Some in the crowd carried signs that read "We Are Sandy Hook. We Choose Love."

"I urge Congress to lead on this issue, and make sure we do everything in our power to keep the guns out of the wrong hands," Soto continued as the crowd cheered.

In the backdrop, the screen showed the number 6,003—the number of people killed by guns since December 14, 2012, according to organizers. After several short speeches the names of each of those 6,003 victims were read aloud.

"Newtown changed America," Senator Richard Blumenthal had declared at the February 27 meeting, but at least as far as gun reform is concerned, the results remain mixed. While Congress's proposals to ban assault weapons and expand background checks for firearm purchases may have fallen short, several states passed related laws of their own in the months following the shooting at Sandy Hook Elementary. During the first six months, five states tightened gun laws: Connecticut, Colorado, New York, Delaware, and Maryland. Meanwhile, fifteen other states have loosened them: Alabama, Arizona, Arkansas, Idaho, Kansas, Kentucky, Maine, Mississippi, Oklahoma, South Dakota, Tennessee, Utah, Virginia, West Virginia, and Wyoming.

Connecticut added more than one hundred guns to the state's list of banned assault weapons. Along with armor-piercing bullets, gun magazines are limited to a capacity of ten rounds. The new law also requires that all firearms sales, including at gun shows, must go through background checks and imposes stiffer penalties for illegal possession and trafficking of guns. The state also created the nation's first registry of people convicted of crimes involving the use, or threat of, dangerous weapons, which will be made available to law enforcement.

Maryland banned the sale of forty-five types of assault weapons and limited magazine capacity to ten rounds. The new law also requires that residents purchasing a handgun must be fingerprinted and go through a safety training course. In Delaware and Colorado, background checks became mandatory for all gun purchases and magazines were limited to a capacity of ten rounds.

New York state passed a sweeping law banning high-capacity magazines, and requiring assault weapons to be registered within the state, including those already owned by residents. All gun buyers must undergo background checks, except transactions among immediate family members. The new law also bans the sale of all assault weapons on the Internet and requires mental health professionals who believe a patient might be a danger to society to report that information to a health care director, who must then relay what they determine to be serious threats to the state Department of Criminal Justice Services.

Still, despite the setbacks, the families remain determined to push forward through the long haul. Those who are part of Sandy Hook Promise believe they have the resolve needed for a fight that they envision might take several years, or even decades. "We know this isn't a sprint. It is a marathon and we intend on keeping this conversation going for as long as it takes. We know it is not going to be easy, but we are a very determined group of people," said Mark Barden.

"I made a promise to Dylan after he died that I would do whatever was in my power to make sure that something like this never happens again," said Nicole Hockley. "I am going to state and local legislators for common sense legislation. There need to be background checks. There need to be magazine limits. There is no need for thirty rounds.

"America has a lot of guns. It always will. No one is going to take those away. All I am asking for is some common sense," Hockley added. "This isn't about politics for me. It is about a promise I made to my son and it is a promise I intend on keeping to prevent these kinds of tragedies from happening again."

CHAPTER 20

———<o>———

A TIME TO HEAL

Twenty days after the shooting, on Thursday, January 3, 2013, the students from Sandy Hook Elementary finally went back to school. Along the way to their new school in nearby Monroe County, students saw handmade greetings and bouquets of balloons in the Sandy Hook green-and-white colors. In the prior week, contractors had been working around the clock to make Chalk Hill Middle School look familiar. When students walked in, they saw the desks arranged in the same patterns and the same posters on the wall.

They were also greeted with a massive police presence. Every car entering the school grounds had to go through a police checkpoint and the driver had to show identification. Bomb-smelling dogs roamed the playground.

On June 21, 2013, the start-of-summer tradition began as yellow school buses departed Chalk Hill Middle School flying colored streamers from their windows, marking the last day of an unimaginably painful school year. While the familiar sights and sounds of joy typical of the last day of school were all around, for Newtown this summer break would be unlike any other. There were the twenty first-graders who wouldn't be making that last bus ride. There were the five educators who wouldn't be packing up their classrooms. Their beloved principal, Dawn Hochsprung, wouldn't be waving to them, but her legacy was scrawled across a school bus window in the form of her favorite words of wisdom: "Be nice to each other. It's really all that matters."

The media had left town long ago, moving on to the next big story, finally giving residents some space to embark on the beginning stages of trying to heal from the precious loss of life, and from the shattered image of a town that had lost its identity to tragedy. For the interconnected web of families, a new normalcy began to take hold. For families with post-traumatic stress disorder, that new normal often means sleepless nights and extra hugs, and lots of counseling.

The family of Carrie Battaglia, including her two children who survived the shooting, is only now beginning to understand the emotional damage inflicted on that day. "My daughter heard everything. She heard the shooting, the pleading, crying, everything," said Battaglia, referring to the sounds coming from Victoria Soto's classroom next door. "You can't undo that.

"She was sure she was going to die," her mother added. "She did not want to die before Christmas."

Her six-year-old daughter now suffers from PTSD. Loud noises frighten her, and in her dreams she often relives that horrible day.

"She's afraid to go to sleep. She has nightmares every night, usually that she is in the school and something is trying to get her, to kill her."

The school day isn't much better. If there is a loud noise, her daughter puts her hands over her ears. The high school provided counselors in the days and weeks afterward. Therapy dogs were brought in, too, but still she is struggling to live a normal life. "If she hears a loud noise she sometimes withdraws. The teachers have to soothe her back," said Battaglia.

Her eight-year-old daughter, a third-grader at the school, has also been affected by the morning of December 14. "Her friends lost their brothers and sisters. She knows she almost lost her sister," said Battaglia. "She has been having a very hard time."

Still, both girls are making progress through regular visits to a trauma specialist at their new school and, in time, their mother hopes the nightmares will end.

For parents, the mental anguish of that day has also had a long-lasting impact beyond what anyone could have expected. Barbara Sibley, who was standing at the school's front door when the shooting began and dove for cover behind a Dumpster, randomly breaks down in tears.

"I always thought post-traumatic stress disorder was for soldiers coming back from war," Barbara said. "It took me a while to accept that I could have it."

It was days before Barbara could shake the chill that entered her body on that December morning. As she gave her account to the

FBI, her husband, Rob, had to keep draping her with heavy blankets, to no avail. She couldn't get warm.

The next week at a local cafe where she was to meet with a co-worker to discuss an upcoming project, she began to experience a panic attack for the first time in her life. "I couldn't function. I felt paralyzed," she recalled.

When her eight-year-old son, Daniel, a third-grader inside Teri Alves's classroom, came home, she remembered him acting normal. Months later, he still suffers from nightmares.

After entering the school, Barbara's husband, Rob, an EMT for the Sandy Hook Volunteer Fire & Rescue Company, who entered the school looking for survivors, still doesn't feel comfortable talking about what he saw that day. "Our lives, our family, will never be the same. Every day it's a new challenge and we have to keep moving forward," Barbara said.

Locally, they are known as "the rebels." The eleven children who survived Victoria Soto's classroom after witnessing the death of their teacher and fellow students will have their own emotional needs as they try to move forward. All have received counseling and several have shown symptoms of severe PTSD. "They are all on the path to healing, but it's been a struggle to say the least," said a class parent in touch with the families.

For the first responders who entered those two classrooms, those images will be with them for the rest of their lives. Several EMTs couldn't go back to work, instead choosing to resign from their jobs. Many were treated for PTSD.

Eric Brown, a lawyer for the union that represents the forty-five members of the Newtown Police Department, believes up to fifteen town police officers who were in that building were in need of medical attention. "We are very concerned about the post-traumatic stress syndrome. For many of these officers, this will be with them for the remainder of their careers," said Brown.

In the days and weeks following December 14, in attempting to deal with the trauma many officers exhausted their holiday time and paid sick leave. For some, the time off wasn't enough to deal with what they had experienced inside the school. "They were forced to go back to work because they have mouths to feed and mortgages to pay," said Brown. One officer decided he wasn't coming back at all, choosing instead to retire.

No one knows what the future holds for these cops, but that day has in many ways defined them. "A lot of these officers are still running on adrenaline. We just don't know what the long-term effects are going to be. These officers aren't the same people today that they were when they woke up on the morning of December fourteenth. That day has become part of who they are now," said Brown.

For everyone affected by the tragedy, the road to recovery may just be beginning. Karen Binder-Brynes, a psychologist who specializes in post-traumatic stress disorder and has worked with families in Newtown, as well as first responders following the terrorist attacks of September 11, 2001, believes that for many the real problems are just beginning to set in. "As time goes by the shock begins to wear off and the permanence of the event just starts to set in and that's when we see the true damage," she said.

In children the signs of PTSD are usually easy to spot. "You have to watch for nonverbal signs that something might be wrong. If your child is experiencing stomachaches, social behavioral changes, or losing interest in things that they were previously interested in, these are signs," Binder-Byrnes explained.

Each child deals with trauma in a very personal way, but often when a child doesn't outwardly express the pain it could lead to further problems, according to Binder-Brynes. "I'm more concerned about the children who experienced the trauma but are holding it in," she said. "They need to have an outlet. The more you can see the distress the more you can react to it.

"It is a very complicated syndrome that has an effect on the biology as well as the psychology. A large portion of these people may never get back to normal, but with proper treatment and time there will be better days ahead."

Members of the clergy are also having trouble moving forward. Many have been under tremendous pressure, as they carry the burden of their parishioners' pain while not paying enough attention to their own grief. Months after the tragedy, the basement at St. Rose of Lima Roman Catholic Church is still full of unopened packages and boxes. The staff had been working diligently to go through all the donations, with postmaster stamps from all around the world, but the sheer amount had proved overwhelming.

"The outpouring of generosity we have seen from around the world is really touching," Father Weiss said.

Seven months removed, Pastor Bob, as he is affectionately known around Newtown, still can't sleep. He has large bags underneath his eyes that betray his easy smile. He is having problems functioning from day to day, but pushes on because he feels he must.

"These families are in so much pain," said Weiss, who has nine families in his parish who lost a child that day. He presided over eight of their funerals in the week following the shooting. He has blocked out much of that day. All that remain are flashes of memories: A little girl calling out his name while sticking her finger through his belt loop as he paced around the firehouse. Driving through the back roads of Newtown at 11 P.M. in a squad car on the way to console the families after receiving final verification that their loved ones were gone. An SUV coming to an abrupt stop in the church parking lot and a dozen out-of-town college kids walking into the church at 3 A.M. to pray the rosary on the morning of December 15.

People looking to him for comfort often ask how something like this can happen in their community. Pastor Bob doesn't have an easy answer, but he believes that as a culture we have strayed from our roots and hopes that the community, and maybe the nation, can use this tragedy to pull closer together. "We have become a culture of death. There is less and less respect for life and the dignity that every person has because we are created by God. There are all these calls for change and new laws but that is not enough.

"Change happens within each one of us and we need to change this attitude that is driving us away from everything that is right and good, everything God intended us to be in this world. We've become too busy for family, too busy for friends, even too busy for God. It's about time that we remember what's really important in life."

In the months that followed the shooting, Father Weiss hasn't been able to take any time off for himself. "The community needs me but I'm struggling, too," he admits, wiping tears from his eyes.

The most painful imprint of all has been left by the children who are never coming back. For these families the pain will never go away.

"Every time there's an event, like the last day of school, it hurts," said Neil Heslin, who lost his son, Jesse. "You keep waiting for it to get easier but it never does."

In Sandy Hook, there is no escaping the agony of that day. Painful reminders are on every light pole, storefront window, and car bumper. Nicole Hockley, who lost her eight-year-old son, Dylan, can't ever escape it. "Every new detail is painful. There hasn't been a day that's gone by where I haven't had to relive it."

Hockley hasn't stopped moving since the day her son's life was taken. She is driven to do everything in her power to make sure no other parent has to endure the pain she feels. "Nothing will bring Dylan back. I know that. We try to live from one moment until the next," said Hockley.

For the families of victims who have chosen to stay out of the media spotlight, a different set of challenges has arisen. For some, frustration grows at the frequent memorials still scattered about the town. "Sometimes, I just want to smash every car I see with a green ribbon," one victim said.

One of the families refuses to walk into the local grocery store where two large green ribbons hang near the front entranceway, another painful reminder. "Everyone wants to help, and I can appreciate that, but how do you begin the process of healing?" the parent said.

Fresh wounds were also opened by a public feud over how to spend the $11 million donated to the United Way in the aftermath of the tragedy.

After a rancorous debate, it was decided that families of each of the twenty-six victims would receive $281,000. Twelve additional families of children who survived the shooting will each get $20,000, while the two teachers who were wounded will receive $150,000 to be split between them.

Local business has also been negatively affected. In the small business enclave at Sandy Hook where Church Hill Road intersects with Glen Road, business was decimated. Two popular local establishments, the Stone River Grille restaurant and the Demitasse cafe, closed their doors within a few months of the tragedy. On January 8, the state approved a $500,000 grant, the maximum allowed, to distribute among Sandy Hook businesses to help the struggling enterprises. Many are skeptical that the town will ever get back to where it was pre–December 14.

Other locals are trying to move on by ignoring the shooting altogether. Many discuss the events as if describing an act of nature that happened to the community without a broader context. The *Newtown Bee* rarely mentions the name Adam Lanza. It is part of a deeper desire to get everything back to how it was before the morning of December 14.

In May, a twenty-eight-member task force of elected officials voted unanimously to recommend that Sandy Hook Elementary

School be demolished. In October, Newtown was allotted $50 million in state funds to rebuild the school. Shortly after, barricades were erected around the structure and security stood guard around as the solemn demolition began. The steel that supported the school's structure was melted down, the bricks and glass were pulverized, and every small remnant hauled away to an undisclosed location until every last trace of Sandy Hook Elementary School was gone.

Questions over how and when to heal is a deeply personal one that is multifaceted. Dr. Carolyn L. Mears, an adjunct professor at the University of Denver and author of *Reclaiming School in the Aftermath of Trauma*, says that the repercussions from tragedies such as Newtown do not begin and end on a single day but are part of an ongoing process. "People want to know when they are going to heal, but there is no answer," said Mears, who is also the parent of two children who survived the shooting at Columbine High School.

"When you are talking about such a wide variety of individuals, each with their own individual experience and traumas, in that regard there is no such thing as a communal healing. There are lots of different processes going on and each one has its own timetable."

The personal path to healing for Mears, who had a life-altering experience and shift of perspective while waiting outside Columbine High School for word that her children had survived, began after she made the decision to internalize life's fragility. "On April twentieth, my world was shattered. I lived in this bubble. I didn't believe something like this could ever happen in my community.

While standing at the school waiting for my son I realized that this was what being human really was, the uncertainty of day to day. It's unnerving but also liberating in a sense of expanded awareness. The whole process of recovery is about accommodating your life story to what has happened to you. Not embracing it, but acknowledging what happened."

Like Columbine, Newtown should expect to go through myriad emotions, which is all part of the process, Mears believes. "As a Columbine mom I can tell you it's a long road. It has its challenges and stumbling blocks but it also has great potential for revealing what is absolutely beautiful about humanity, that transformative nature of trauma. It can be very positive but also, in some cases, it can never be resolved. Some of the long-lasting damage will be irreversible.

"The community image of Littletown and Columbine were shattered. In Newtown, there is a group identity that has been shattered. Reestablishing who you are, as in, as individuals, is extremely important. There will be periods of controversies, divisiveness, and anger, all of which are symptomatic of a trauma response."

Fifteen years later people will still look at her driver's license and mention Columbine to her, bringing back painful memories. Over time the memories begin to fade and the news cycle begins to move on, but for the community a type of permanence attaches itself to each person. In time, new challenges arise as many of the students who experienced the shooting at Columbine have families of their own and children heading off to their first day of school. She says that, united by a shared experience, the trauma breeds a stronger communal bond that most people can never understand.

"Over the passage of time we worry less, but we are always aware. I am a Columbine mom and I always will be. That is something I realized I had to live with. It's part of my identity."

Then there is the inevitable branding that happens to a town that is the scene of a mass tragedy. On December 14, Newtown joined an exclusive club with Virginia Tech, Aurora, and, of course, Columbine as communities associated with tragedy.

"Newtown took what happened in Columbine and brought it to the next level. We are talking about babies that were killed. It is a whole new level of horror. We didn't want our community and school to become synonymous with mass shootings and tragedy but we didn't have a choice, and unfortunately, neither will Newtown," said Mears.

"For Columbine, the tragedy may have begun on April twenty, but it didn't end that day. It goes on until this day. In Newtown, in many ways December fourteen is forever."

In Newtown, First Selectman Pat Llodra is determined to move her community forward. After months of memorials, benefit concerts, gifts, and donations, in July Llodra announced that the town will no longer accept nonlocally sponsored donations. "We are very grateful, but it was time for us to get back to living our lives and our normal routines," Llodra explained. Unlike other towns where mass tragedies have occurred, Newtown will not be hosting any public memorials on the one year anniversary of the shooting. The municipality has requested privacy.

Llodra recognizes that the tragedy in her hometown has changed the country in ways that may not always be easy to quantify. "This horrible event changed our social fabric in ways that aren't always easy to see on the surface," she said. "The policy changes will come in time, but it is also more, something greater than that.

"Every time something like this happens, it makes us kinder people. We become less quick to criticize. We become a little more open-minded."

She insists that Newtown will not be negatively "branded" because the people will refuse to allow themselves to be defined by the "act of one evil person."

"I truly believe the world sees us not for the horrible thing that happened to us, but for the subsequent acts of love that followed," Llodra said. "We will never forget but we will survive, and we will thrive again."

AFTERWORD

Over time, the memorials and shrines that once dominated Sandy Hook began to disappear. Left alone with their grief, the residents of Newtown have struggled with the same questions the rest of the country started asking after the morning of December 14. Why did Adam Lanza shoot his mother before going to Sandy Hook Elementary School and shooting twenty children and six educators before turning the gun on himself? And what can be done to prevent it from ever happening again?

As the search for answers continued, one question began to haunt the community more than the others: What could they have done to change the trajectory of that day? What if . . .

What if someone had intervened and stopped the bullying?
While at Sandy Hook Elementary School, Nancy Lanza believed her son's Asperger's syndrome and sensory perception disorder

made him a target for bullies. She tried changing schools and was a frequent presence at school functions and meetings, but no matter how often she complained to faculty and staff, she believed no one was looking out for her fragile son.

"They tell me what they think I want to hear but no one wants to invest the time to make sure he is safe," Nancy told one friend.

What if Richard Novia had stayed at Newtown High School?
Nancy believed she had finally found an advocate at Newtown High School in the tech club's adviser Richard Novia. The teacher saw potential in the bright young boy. During his freshman year, he studied Adam's condition and took him under his wing. As a sophomore it appeared that Adam was making progress.

But before Adam was to enter his junior year, Novia announced he was leaving. Nancy was devastated, fearing her son's only protector would now be gone. Against Novia's warnings, Nancy pulled Adam out of Newtown High School. The boy had two brief stints at college but never found the safety net that he had at the high school.

"I think about the 'what ifs' more than I'd like to admit," Novia said, after a long pause. "Maybe things would have been different. I guess we will never know.

"I think Adam did what he did because he was angry at the school and wanted everyone to know," Novia added. "His mother believed the school had failed him. It was all he had. When that was gone, he lost everything. He just sat alone in that house all day and all night."

What if neighbors had taken more of an interest in what was going on behind the closed doors at the Lanza house?

Looking back, many neighbors now ask themselves if there was more they could have done to reach out to the Lanza family. While most residents were friendly, 36 Yogananda Street seemed like a black sheep in the neighborhood. Inside the house, Adam Lanza was sitting alone in his darkened room, hour after hour, immersed in the world of violent video games and online obsessively researching mass killers and the military. He cut off all communication with his father and brother, and as his mother began to travel more, Adam lived in complete isolation. Perhaps, many wondered, if they had just reached out, offered one kind gesture, one word of reassurance, maybe the tragedy could have been prevented?

"We all just went about our business," one neighbor said. "I wish I could go back and reach out. I know a lot of us do."

"Looking back there were signs that something was wrong inside that house but none of us took the time to offer real help," another neighbor added.

What if Adam hadn't had access to the ultraviolent images?

Thirty years ago, a person living in self-imposed seclusion like Adam Lanza would have been incapable of immersing himself so easily in the study of weapons and in mastering first-person shooting games. Today, all of the information and practical training is readily available at the click of a mouse or press of a button.

"It's hard to imagine an Adam Lanza existing a century ago, before there was this culture of violence and depravity," said Dr. Edward Shorter, the professor of the history of medicine and psychiatry in the Faculty of Medicine of the University of Toronto.

What if Adam didn't have access to high-powered weaponry?
Stronger gun laws would not have stopped Adam Lanza from walking into Sandy Hook Elementary School. Under Connecticut's current legislation, it was already illegal for Adam, at the age of twenty, to own a firearm. But today more people have access to more powerful firearms that either didn't exist fifty years ago or were not readily available.

"These assault weapons today are so powerful and destructive," said Nicole Hockley. "Perhaps it is time to ask the question, why do all these people need to have such powerful weapons?"

Still, most of the "what ifs" fall on Nancy Lanza, who is no longer around to defend herself: What if Nancy Lanza, who knew her son was mentally ill and had seen his collection of violent images, hadn't stockpiled her home with weapons? What if she hadn't left her mentally ill son alone for weeks at a time? Or as Mark Barden, who lost his son Daniel at Sandy Hook, poignantly asked: What if Nancy Lanza had chosen a different hobby for her mentally ill son?

In hindsight, any number of "what ifs" or interventions could have been made during the chain of events leading up to the morning of December 14 that might have prevented the tragedy from unfolding. Yet no one scenario offers complete reassurance that history would have taken an entirely different course.

What if Peter and Nancy had stayed together? What if . . . What if . . .

The question moving forward is: How does society stop another massacre like this from ever happening again, especially given that mass shootings have occurred with such frequency in recent years that the phenomenon almost resembles an epidemic?

Despite the best efforts of lawmakers, no single piece of legislation could have prevented the Newtown tragedy and no single act can be reasonably trusted to safeguard against future acts of violence. Some believe the search for a solution will be found in the field of science.

Dr. Jeremy Richman, who lost his daughter Avielle at Sandy Hook, thinks future mass killings can be prevented by studying brain health. "These terrible tragedies happen all over the country," he said. "Not only in schools, but in parks, places of worship, really anywhere. Each time the country responds in the same way, calling for improvements in school safety, gun legislation, and mental health. All three need to be dealt with, but with mental health we never get anywhere. We need to understand the pathologies, the things in their brains that go wrong. We need to understand it and prevent it."

The Richman family founded the Avielle Foundation in the wake of their daughter's death. It is funded through donations and grants and hopes to remove the stigma for people seeking mental health aid, develop the concept of a "brain health checkup," and identify behavioral and biochemical diagnostics for detection of people at risk of violent behaviors. Richman, a researcher at the pharmaceutical company Boehringer Ingelheim, has extensive research experience that spans neuroscience to neuropsychopharmacology. His wife, Jennifer Hensel, is a medical writer with her own company.

"Our immediate response to what happened to our daughter was that we had to do something about this so people don't have to face what we are facing ever again," Richman said. "We believe that starts with erasing society's stigma and misperceptions about brain health. If you are told your child is psychotic and that child is labeled psychotic, there is nothing you can do and as a parent you are going to be in denial. It's scary not to have hope. But if your child is diagnosed with diabetes or nut allergies, it's something we can wrap our arms around and everyone wants to help."

Richman hopes his foundation will enable people to see mental health issues in the same vein as they do more traditionally treated physical problems. "If you are diagnosed with too much dopamine, and as a result have trouble with impulse control, that's not overwhelming," he explained. "That can be dealt with."

Richman wants to see the country shift from mental health to brain health and believes the language itself is counterproductive to helping those who are afflicted. "No doctor would look at your broken arm and call you a broken arm," Richman said. "You are not your disease."

What if Adam's Asperger's syndrome and sensory perception disorder had been properly treated?

From early childhood, it was clear to those around him that Adam Lanza was a deeply disturbed young man. While still in elementary school, he was diagnosed with mental illness. Always an outsider, he was prone to isolation and saw the world differently from his peers. His journals were filled with violent drawings, some of which were discovered by his school and his mother. Many of them can be seen as warning signs of potential future violence.

"It was obvious that Adam was not well and wasn't getting the care he needed," said Richman. "Once we know what to look for, we can treat these people."

Shortly after starting the Avielle Foundation, the Richmans were shocked by the outpouring of support they received. Messages began to flood in from parents around the country, all in need of support in coping with their children's violent tendencies.

In reality, none of these solutions might work. In life, people are free to make choices. Nancy Lanza made her choices. Adam made his. This has led some people to choose a simpler explanation for what happened on the morning of December 14—evil. In a planet that is inhabited by seven billion people, no matter how society or culture evolves, a small percentage of those people will always make decisions to commit senseless and seemingly random, unspeakably horrific acts.

"For as long as we have walked the earth, there have always been acts of evil and there always will be," said Monsignor Robert Weiss.

In confronting a tragedy so unfathomably terrible, people have a need to seek out a reasonable explanation for the senseless loss of life. Attaching a label to it gives back a feeling of control. Without an answer to the question of why, communities are left facing the random chaos of life. They are forced to face the realization that in a world with so many moving parts, it is impossible to have control over random events and tragedies. It leaves open the possibility that what happened at Sandy Hook could happen one day at their child's school. It is an uncomfortably reality and one which forces the search for an explanation to go on.

"We have to keep looking for answers. We must keep examining these issues. The conversation must continue," said Mary Ellen O'Toole, the former criminal profiler for the FBI who has studied mass killers. "The moment we stop asking why is the very moment we give up the future to the next mass killer, who is out there now plotting. We can't stop believing that we have the power to stop it from happening again. We can't sit back and just let it occur. The randomness has to be explored because we have to know why.

"We may never get to one final answer, but we have to keep trying."

ACKNOWLEDGMENTS

This book is only possible because of those who graciously shared their stories with me, including families of the victims, survivors, first responders, and friends and family of the Lanzas. Thank you all.

It was the tireless work of my literary agent Sharlene Martin of Martin Literary Management who believed this was an important story that needed to be told and worked hard to make this book possible. Thank you, Sharlene.

I cannot say enough about the professionalism and expertise exhibited by my editor Tricia Boczkowski and the entire team at Simon & Schuster's Gallery Books—Jen Bergstrom, Louise Burke, Jen Robinson, Elana Cohen—an amazing group of people.

I've had many great editors over the years who have all contributed to this book coming to fruition; JoAnne Wasserman, Kirsten Danis, and Robert F. Moore of the New York *Daily News*.

I also owe a debt of gratitude to several other people. Chelsia

ACKNOWLEDGMENTS

Rose Marcius, a great journalist, writer, and friend who helped read through my copy and gave me inspiration in the fragile early days while I was trying to get this project off the ground. Dave Crawford, my seventh-grade English teacher at Danville Middle School, who helped preserve enough of my curiosity to get me through the most boring years of my life (middle school). New York City journalist and author Christina Boyle, whose expert eyes helped me with the manuscript.

My family was also instrumental in the completion of this book. My parents, Gina and Arthur Lysiak, and my mother-in-law Candace Belles, and John Thrash, who all generously opened up their home to my family during my months away in Newtown.

I also want to thank my daughters, Isabel, Hilde, and Georgia Lysiak, who understand that having a dad who is a reporter often leads to an unconventional childhood but always seem to effortlessly roll with it, and my wife, Bridget Lysiak, whose seemingly pathological pursuit to always better herself has proven contagious.